Praise for **NO STORM LASTS FOREVER**

*"No Storm Lasts Forever will rekindle your belief
in the human spirit. Terry Gordon and his amazing
family show us how to thrive even against an
immeasurable, seemingly unbeatable adversary."*

— **Kenny Loggins**

*"No Storm Lasts Forever is both heartbreaking and
triumphant. It is one father's courageous account of personal
tragedy—his son's spinal cord injury and resultant paralysis.
The reader's initial response is one of compassion and empathy.
As the story progresses, this turns into a sense of triumph
as the author grows to accept what his God has ordained,
making use of his sorrow to enter a new life of love and faith."*

— **Richard Selzer, M.D.,** retired surgeon and
author of *Confessions of a Knife*

*"I was very moved by No Storm Lasts Forever. It's so
rare that a father, in the midst of such tragedy, can grow
so fully and then write about it so clearly. His message that
the worst suffering calls forth the most compassion is the
central one to our human existence. The question isn't about
suffering. It's how we walk through it, who we walk with,
and who we walk for—in shared spirit. No Storm Lasts
Forever is a fine book, written with heart and head,
and teaches us the healing power of nature."*

— **Samuel Shem,** author of *The House of God*

NO
STORM
LASTS
FOREVER

Hay House Titles of Related Interest

YOU CAN HEAL YOUR LIFE, the movie,
starring Louise L. Hay & Friends
(available as a 1-DVD program and an expanded 2-DVD set)
Watch the trailer at: **www.LouiseHayMovie.com**

THE SHIFT, the movie,
starring Dr Wayne W. Dyer
(available as a 1-DVD program and an expanded 2-DVD set)
Watch the trailer at: **www.DyerMovie.com**

*A DAILY DOSE OF SANITY: A Five-Minute Soul Recharge
for Every Day of the Year,* by Alan Cohen

*THE GIFT OF FIRE: How I Made Adversity
Work for Me,* by Dan Caro

*HEALING WITH THE ANGELS: How the Angels Can Assist
You in Every Area of Your Life,* by Doreen Virtue

WISHES FULFILLED: Mastering the Art of Manifesting,
by Dr Wayne W. Dyer

YOU CAN CREATE AN EXCEPTIONAL LIFE,
by Louise Hay & Cheryl Richardson

All of the above are available at your local
bookstore, or may be ordered by visiting:

Hay House UK: **www.hayhouse.co.uk**
Hay House USA: **www.hayhouse.com**®
Hay House Australia: **www.hayhouse.com.au**
Hay House South Africa: **www.hayhouse.co.za**
Hay House India: **www.hayhouse.co.in**

NO STORM LASTS FOREVER

Transforming Suffering Into Insight

DR. TERRY A. GORDON

HAY HOUSE

Australia • Canada • Hong Kong • India
South Africa • United Kingdom • United States

First published and distributed in the United Kingdom by:
Hay House UK Ltd, 292B Kensal Rd, London W10 5BE. Tel.: (44) 20 8962 1230;
Fax: (44) 20 8962 1239. www.hayhouse.co.uk

Published and distributed in the United States of America by:
Hay House, Inc., PO Box 5100, Carlsbad, CA 92018-5100. Tel.: (1) 760 431 7695 or
(800) 654 5126; Fax: (1) 760 431 6948 or (800) 650 5115. www.hayhouse.com

Published and distributed in Australia by:
Hay House Australia Ltd, 18/36 Ralph St, Alexandria NSW 2015. Tel.: (61) 2 9669
4299; Fax: (61) 2 9669 4144. www.hayhouse.com.au

Published and distributed in the Republic of South Africa by:
Hay House SA (Pty), Ltd, PO Box 990, Witkoppen 2068. Tel./Fax: (27) 11 467
8904. www.hayhouse.co.za

Published and distributed in India by:
Hay House Publishers India, Muskaan Complex, Plot No.3, B-2, Vasant Kunj, New
Delhi – 110 070. Tel.: (91) 11 4176 1620; Fax: (91) 11 4176 1630.
www.hayhouse.co.in

Distributed in Canada by:
Raincoast, 9050 Shaughnessy St, Vancouver, BC V6P 6E5. Tel.: (1) 604 323 7100;
Fax: (1) 604 323 2600

CONTENTS

Acknowledgments. ix
Foreword by Dr. Wayne W. Dyer xi
Preface. xvii

PART I: The Gathering Storm

Clouds Across the Moon 3
The Thunder Rolls 6
The Journey Begins 10
The Hand That Rocks the Cradle 15
I'll Be There 19

PART II: The Sky Is Crying

Give Me the Good News. 25
Do You Believe in Magic? 29
Beauty and the Beast. 35
Reach the Summit. 38
Here Comes the Sun 44
Hey God, Where Are You?. 48
A Song of Birth 52
The Rain Don't Last 58
Rejuvenation 62
An Angel Passing Through My Room 67
I'm Goin' Home. 72
You'll Never Walk Alone. 76
But for the Grace of God. 80
Hiding Underwater 84
Patience and Hope 88

The Road Less Traveled 92
Lessons Learned 96
He Ain't Heavy, He's My Brother 103
Man of Steel 108
Losing Balance. 112
Running Blind 115
Where Is the Love? 119
Ease On Down the Road 122
Nothin' Ever Lasts Forever. 126
Healing Hands. 130
Renegade 133
Strong Enough to Bend. 136
Rainbow Connection. 139
A Change Is Coming 145
Swimming Upstream. 148
Two Wolves. 151

PART III: The Sunshine's Dancing on the Clouds

A New Beginning 157
A Time for Everything 161
Don't It Make My Brown Eyes Blue? 165
A Walk in the Park 170
Gratitude. 174
K-I-S-S 178
I'll Be Home for Christmas. 181
Does Anybody Really Know What Time It Is?. 185
Magic Carpet Ride. 189
Letting Go. 192
Celebrate Me Home 197

Epilogue. 205
About the Author 207

ACKNOWLEDGMENTS

Life has a way of preparing us for what is yet to come. These lessons, if we choose to accept them, can offer us the tools with which to navigate the experience. I have been blessed by many people, coming from all walks of life, who have entered my life at just the right moment to offer their wisdom. To each of these sages, for each contribution to the mosaic of my life, I am forever grateful.

To my wife, Angela, my Bashert, who has gently coaxed me onto the path: the patience, love, and latitude you have selflessly granted has empowered me to do what you have so masterfully done your entire life: serve others.

To Art Blair: a kindred spirit whose crystal-hazel eyes showed me not only the portal to a beautiful soul but also a pathway to heaven.

To Bob Ligon, L.Ac., practitioner of Chinese Medicine and Acupuncture: your wisdom and counsel have enriched my mind, body, and spirit beyond imagination.

To Jennifer Shoe: although well on your way back home, you continue to inspire.

To Kenny Loggins: your music has for years touched the deepest recesses of my soul. I am forever grateful that the Universe orchestrated our paths to intersect in that small airport in Louisiana. Your insightful lyrics, my friend, have inspired this father beyond words.

To my brother, Dr. Wayne W. Dyer: you are the consummate healer. I am but one of millions of recipients who have been blessed by the purity of your insight. Your guidance has helped prepare me for this life's journey. Thank you. Thank you.

And last but certainly not least, to Tyler: the love letters scribed here are for you, son. In many ways, you are the man I strive to become. The lessons I have learned from this experience and from you have forever changed me. My sincerest prayer is that one day these pages might in some small way help you as your life's journey continues to unfold. God's speed to you, Ty . . .

FOREWORD

This is a story about love. A truly magnificent story, written by a man whom I consider to be one of the finest human beings I have ever been blessed to know, and whom I am so proud to call a friend and colleague. This book is far more than a collection of highly emotional, skillfully written essays detailing a journey through the darkness of an almost unspeakably horrific accident—and the impact of such a tragedy on a father and son and an entire family. And this book is not just about how to weather a severe storm or how to come to grips with such an incident in one's life. The book you hold in your hands is one of the most beautiful love stories I have ever read.

Dr. Terry Gordon, a brilliant cardiologist, has spent the better part of his adult life smack-dab in the middle of crises. He has been right there, often working feverishly throughout the night without any sleep for days, simply doing what he vowed to do when he took the Hippocratic oath. He is an accomplished member of the healing profession, a dedicated man who has been in awe of the heart and its majestic role in all of our lives.

The symbol of the heart ♥ is the symbol of love. It has an intelligence all its own. And when we point to ourselves, we always place our finger right there on our heart, not at our head. And no one ever refers to his or her beloved as "my sweet*head*"; it is always "my sweetheart."

It is no surprise that Terry chose to become as intimately connected and knowledgeable about this space of love in the middle of our chest that is simply called our *heart*. Terry is indeed a man of love. His dedication to his patients, and to keeping them as heart-healthy as possible, is what has defined this man. It was this aura of love surrounding Terry that drew me to him in the first place—and it was this love energy that prompted me to encourage him to write this story and to have it published by Hay House, an organization that is synchronized with the spiritual heartbeat of the human race, and a place that I have called home now for many years.

DR. TERRY GORDON IS A HEART SPECIALIST in every sense of the word. He was very moved after viewing a video of a young boy named Josh Miller, who died on a football field simply because the school did not have a device on the sideline that could have saved his life. Josh's heart could've been reactivated with a portable machine called an *automated external defibrillator,* or an AED. Terry saw this tragic event as an opportunity, much like he demonstrates in each and every chapter of this wonderful book.

With Terry's dogged determination, he was instrumental in having 4,500 AED devices placed in schools throughout the state of Ohio, where he practiced medicine as a cardiologist. He also pushed to have thousands of people trained in how to use these machines to save the lives of young athletes who suffer from sudden cardiac arrest, generally at sporting events. For his efforts, Dr. Terry Gordon was recognized by the American Heart Association as the National Physician of the Year in 2002. And today, Terry works tirelessly to get The Josh Miller HEARTS Act passed at the national level to fund a program to have AEDs placed in every school in America.

Every time Terry hears of another young person losing his or her life unnecessarily because this equipment is unavailable, he first cries inside and then goes to work, doing what he can to make a difference. He will call me and ask if I know of any way we can bring this issue to the forefront of America's conscience. Young people dying because we are slumbering at the switch is simply intolerable. Terry is a man of the heart, a man of love, and his mission today is to get those in positions of power to awaken. He asks, "How can we allow such a condition to exist and defend it by saying we don't have the funds? They can fund wars so readily; why not find those hidden dollars and use them to save the lives of hundreds of young people who die needlessly?"

I feel Terry's passion for keeping the hearts of young people beating. In fact, when I introduced him to my practice of Bikram yoga several years ago, his first response was, "This is a hot studio, and it needs to have an AED in the place in the event that someone's heart should stop suddenly while doing this kind of intense exercising." Now here is a portrait of the man whose book you hold in your hand: Terry, at his own expense, purchased an AED for the studio on Maui where I practice and arranged for the instructors and myself to be trained in how to use one of these devices in the event of an emergency. This is a man of passion, a man of the heart, a man who lives what he writes about.

A FEW YEARS BACK, TERRY WAS SCHEDULED to accompany me on a cruise to Alaska, where I was lecturing on the ship as a part of a large conference at sea sponsored by Hay House. Just a couple of weeks prior to our departure from Seattle, I received the devastating news from Terry that his young son, Tyler, had been involved in a very serious automobile accident, and that it was quite likely that there was a severe spinal-cord injury involved. Terry immediately flew to Colorado to be with Tyler, and of course he was forced to cancel the plans we had for his trip to Alaska.

This book you are now about to read is Terry's account of the magic transition that his family was asked to experience. Here you will see firsthand the heart I have been describing in the Foreword to this compelling book. This is not a sad story; in fact, every time I reread any of the passages, I find myself experiencing an overall sense of well-being with a deeper connection to my own source of being.

I have written and spoken many times of the great mysteries of the universe. I have frequently proclaimed that there are no accidents in this universe and that all of us, no exceptions, are not human beings having a spiritual experience. Rather, the reverse is my truth: we are all infinite spiritual beings having a temporary human experience.

Terry's beautifully written journal entries reinforce the idea that peace and infinite love can be found in the most formidable and burdensome moments of our lives. From the esteemed perspective of a poet, Terry reveals the depth of his love for his son and is able to convey to all of us how to find our own boundless love for the spirit in circumstances that otherwise drive so many into chagrin and, ultimately, defeat. All of these many years of treating broken hearts were preparation for Terry to learn how to treat and repair his own.

Many times while reading Terry's words, I wept. Not tears of sadness; rather, they were appreciative tears of gratitude for reminding me of a truth I have attempted to teach for all of my own adult life. That is, when you change the way you look at things, the things you look at change.

Thank you, Terry, for reminding me so splendidly that an enlightened life is not about avoiding the rainstorms, but learning how to find peace and divine love in the midst of the storm. This is really a book about alchemy. It is not about waiting for the storm to pass; instead, it is about converting the storm to inner peace and spiritual awakening.

I love this book, and I love you, Dr. Terry Gordon. And I send you all of my blessings, Tyler Gordon. God bless you.

Namaste,
Dr. Wayne W. Dyer

PREFACE

*"We are not what we know but
what we are willing to learn."*
— MARY CATHERINE BATESON

My dear gentles,

Life is not a random set of experiences; it is a learning curve. At each level we are offered potential lessons. From the encounter, we may choose to gain insight and progress on to a higher path, or we may decide to ignore the experience and remain stagnant. Either way, we will be tested. If we fail to learn from the instruction provided, it will be offered to us in some fashion again and again until such time that we finally get it.

What we are to learn doesn't necessarily become fully apparent at first glance; it may take time and only be understood with clarity once more pieces are added to the puzzle.

I once held the belief that my spiritual development was something I could put on the back burner of life. I assumed that I would tap into it down the road when I have the luxury of more time. I looked forward to that, anticipating being able to nurture my spirituality once everything else settled in to a comfortable place. I have since changed my mind.

Recently, circumstances unfolding in my life have resulted in a shift in the paradigm of my thought. I now appreciate that my spiritual development is of critical importance. Its evolution is something not to be delayed until the tomorrows of life. The advancement of my spiritual awakening has become not only a desire; it has taken on the priority of being essential for my very survival.

As a physician who on a daily basis dealt with life-and-death circumstances, I understand that our existence in its present form is tenuous at best. Its course can be altered in an instant.

Having experienced firsthand such a dramatic change, I have been challenged to lead my family through a quagmire of immense suffering.

My wife, Angela, and I worked very hard to raise our four children, nurturing them in an environment filled with love. Our hopes and dreams for them were what every parent wishes for their children: stability in their world, happiness in their lives, and most important, peace in their hearts.

Life was perfect! Our three daughters—Mattie-Rose, Laila, and Britt—had graduated from college with degrees in education. Our son, Tyler, was enrolled at Fort Lewis College in Durango, Colorado, having just completed his sophomore year studying business.

Then just when we thought we had it all figured out, we were thrown a curveball. Life as we knew it came crashing down.

The pages that follow offer a journaling of the experience. I have never kept a diary; I always thought it was silly to write something about myself that's so private and revealing. I assumed that the underlying reason others did catalog their feelings was the subconscious hope that someone else would discover their words.

When first suggested to me, I quite frankly dismissed the idea of journaling. But I must share with you that when our tragic event occurred I initially found it extremely difficult to talk about. I needed the time in order to allow the experience to be absorbed into the deepest recesses of my soul, where it would be pondered over and over again. It would be in that silent space that I would search for meaning.

No Storm Lasts Forever will offer you insight into my deepest thoughts as I navigated through this tumultuous trek. When I first began the process of expressing in words my journey, I soon found that one thought would trigger another. On occasion, they would lead me on a tangential path, only to find that I had been taken to a place I may not have found had I not placed my thoughts in written form.

Journaling also allowed me to distill my ideas down to the most elemental level, then to expand on them, exploring places deep within that I had never before recognized. It provided me with incredible clarity in the midst of the chaos I was experiencing. Once completed, the journal imparted to me an unencumbered view of the whole process, revealing the progress I had made along this, at times, dreadful path. Writing enabled me to explore my thoughts and feelings in the pursuit of relieving the most profound pain and suffering I had ever experienced. I grew along the way—and for that, I am profoundly grateful.

The result of my self-exploration and the discoveries made along the way were nothing short of miraculous. The process turned out to be extremely therapeutic for me. And as an added bonus, journaling saved me a lot of money I would have wasted on expensive psychoanalysis!

When my journals were shared with a few of my closest friends, it was suggested that I share my inner thoughts with others, so that those in pain might benefit from my experience. As such, I humbly offer this to you.

The format of *No Storm Lasts Forever* is presented in three parts. "Part I: The Gathering Storm" will set the stage for the journal entries that will follow in "Part II: The Sky Is Crying" and "Part III: The Sunshine's Dancing on the Clouds."

If you are looking for a story with an ending in which everyone lives happily ever after, I would suggest that you close this book right away and try to get your money back. Because you see, our story is far from complete. If, on the other hand, you find yourself searching for hope in the midst of whatever tragedy you find yourself in, my sincere prayer is that *No Storm Lasts Forever* will help you find what it is that we all seek: shalom, salaam, peace.

The pages that follow are not meant to imply that I am enlightened. The truth is quite the opposite. What I believe is that through the grace of God, I have been granted a glimpse of what that might be!

Namaste,
Dr. Terry A. Gordon

PART I

THE GATHERING STORM

CLOUDS ACROSS THE MOON

(June 29th, 2009)

It was early evening, and the sun had already set. I was upstairs in my office when my daughter Mattie-Rose arrived home from Chicago. She had been living there for a year or so teaching at an inner-city elementary school. We shared our usual reunion hugs and kisses, but something felt strangely hesitant about her embrace. As a parent, there is this sixth sense one gets when it comes to your children, and although she attempted to hide it, I could tell that something was amiss. I could feel she was weighed down by a heavy sadness.

3

"What's up, sweetie?" I asked as she sat down at my feet, her arms resting on my knees.

"Well, Da Da," she replied, "I always thought that the older I got, the more control I would gain over my life." Her eyes brimming with tears, she continued, "But it just seems like the farther along I go, the more difficult life is becoming for me." As a single tear trickled down her cheek, she sighed and said, "I just assumed it would get easier."

Pulling her up from the floor and onto my lap, we embraced. I began slowly rocking her back and forth as I had done so many times when she was younger. Silence intervened as I began to gather my thoughts; I knew that my response would be an important one for her. As I pondered her comments, I looked out the window of my office and saw a half-moon chiseled into the darkness of night, noticing a small sliver of it obstructed from view by a lone cloud.

"You know, darling," I began, "I don't think that's how it's supposed to be. If we are to progress in life, likely it will get more difficult. But the more daunting the challenges and the greater the apparent obstacles, the more potential there is for personal growth. There is an ancient mystical text of Judaism called the Kabbalah, which tells us that the falls of our life provide us with the energy to propel ourselves to a much higher level.

"It would be wonderful if we could pass through this life without any problems. It would be nice to avoid sorrow, sadness, disease, and even death, but we can't. Such is life, honey. None of us is immune. At some time or another, we will all endure these seemingly negative experiences. The question becomes, are they really negative experiences?

"When adversity comes, it's how we respond to that difficulty that determines who we are. Our life experiences become calamities only if we make the conscious decision to make tragedies out of them. We might just as easily choose to view them as opportunities for personal growth. The difficulties we experience can become the driving force of change.

"Rather than lamenting so-called adversities, we can choose to be *grateful* for them. We can embrace them and accept them as gifts from the Divine, knowing that within them lie the lessons that can promote our development and maturation. By being grateful for adversity, we can use it as an opportunity to transform turmoil, disappointment, or suffering into understanding, insight, or resolve."

I left her with that thought as I gently kissed her forehead.

THE THUNDER ROLLS

(6:40 the following morning . . .)

One of the worst phone calls a parent could imagine awakened me. A grave voice on the other end of the line informed me that our son, Tyler, had been involved in an automobile accident. Tyler was in the Mercy Regional Medical Center emergency room in Durango, Colorado, and had sustained a significant neck injury that had damaged his spinal cord. Then the dreaded words were hesitantly spoken: "Your son is quadriplegic."

As the impact of the words sank in, the physician and the objective scientist in me kicked into gear. I knew Ty would require emergency surgery to stabilize his fractured neck to prevent any further damage to his spinal cord. The medical flight was already on its way to Durango to pick up its precious cargo and transfer him to Swedish Medical Center in Denver.

I must get to our son! Within an hour of the shocking news, I had hurriedly packed a bag and bolted from our home. Ten minutes down the road, it hit me that I had just left my wife wailing. Wailing! Tears welled up in my eyes as I thought, *Angela, I am so sorry.* In my haste, I didn't take the time to comfort my beloved partner at a time when she needed me the most. I had to get to Denver to be with our son, but oh how I wish I could relive that moment of departure. How I wish I could have a second chance to comfort my wife. *Angela, please forgive me. Please forgive me.*

The next flight to Denver was overbooked, yet miraculously I ended up with a seat. In three hours, I'd be there. Seated by a window, I felt caged and helpless. My mind was crazed. The chaotic frenzy of thoughts banging inside my head was almost unbearable. Now incommunicado, I didn't know if our son was alive or dead, brain damaged or hemorrhaging from multiple injuries. Where was he? Had the helicopter made it to Durango? Did the life flight make the trip to Denver safely? I thought: *Tyler, son, are you okay? Pops will be there as soon as he can.*

As I peered out the window, I saw muted gray clouds. While staring into the murky sky, dark speckles appeared. At first I assumed it was an optical illusion, but the black speckles persisted and steadily increased in number, coalescing into small clumps. I rubbed my eyes, but the spots wouldn't go away. I closed my eyes, but they remained in view.

My mind reeled with horrible projections of Tyler's condition. What would I find when I finally got to the hospital? Would I make it there in time to see him before they rushed him into surgery? Would he recognize me? I needed to see him, to tell him how very much I love him. I wanted him to see me, to know that I was there with him and that he would be okay. *Would* he be okay? *Please God; help me get there in time,* I begged. *Help me help my son. Help me help my family. Help me be strong. Help me. . . . Help.*

I prayed. I prayed deeper than ever before. I felt myself falling from a high jagged cliff and my descent rapidly accelerating. The loud rush of the cold wind was deafening. I looked down, frightened by a sinking feeling and the darkness below. *God, please help. I ask this not for me, but for those I love.*

It was subtle when it occurred. The sound of the whooshing wind came to a gentle halt as a protective cocoon of white noise surrounded me, strand by strand.

I found myself in a place of unfathomable peace. I felt the Presence. I cannot recall if I actually heard the message in words or if I perceived them from deep within, but the meaning was clear when it said: "Terry, just yesterday you gave your daughter soothing counsel. You shared your truth with her. You can talk the talk. But now, you must live it. Know that there are no mistakes. Everything is in perfect order . . . even this."

I remember questioning whether I had the strength to do this. The answer was clear: "You *can* do this."

But, dear God, how? How do I proceed?

By Divine inspiration, the way became clear: "Treat this as if you had chosen it to be."

I repeated aloud, "As if I had *chosen* it to be . . ."

I was being offered a choice. I could continue on the same familiar path I had walked for years, or I could choose a new way of seeing experiences, a different way of interpreting adversity. A gift had been offered. Placed before me was a tool I could use to transform suffering into insight. I didn't quite understand it, but I felt a strange sense that I had just been blessed.

THE JOURNEY BEGINS

(June 30th)

The moment the airplane touched down in Denver, I turned on my cell phone to find a single voice-mail message. It was from Dr. Zaki Ibrahim, a trauma surgeon at Swedish Hospital. His gentle voice confirmed that Tyler had arrived safely. He also informed me that emergent surgery was planned for 2:30 P.M. that day, and that I was to call him upon my arrival at the hospital. I had made it in time!

When I entered the hospital, I went directly to the intensive-care unit. As I entered his room, I found Ty resting, his breathing somewhat labored and forced. The nurse told me that he had been heavily sedated. I leaned over the bed rail and gently kissed his forehead. "I love you very much, son. I'm here with you,

Boosle Boy." This nickname for him had stuck when, as a youngster, he was referred to by us as our "beautiful boy." His pronunciation at that age was "Boosle Boy."

The first groggy words out of his mouth were: "I told them not to bother you guys." Indeed, he had told the physicians in Durango not to call us. And guess what? They didn't! HIPAA (the Health Insurance Portability and Accountability Act) sucks, as its regulations prevent the release of medical information unless a patient gives permission. Even though I was a physician myself, I couldn't get a doctor in the ER in Durango to speak to me about Tyler's condition, critical as it was.

The good news was that Tyler was alive. His neck had been shattered, but there were no other apparent injuries. It is difficult to describe the bifurcated feelings of joy and despair I simultaneously experienced observing what Tyler could do physically, and at the same moment realizing what he could not. Yes, he was alive, but his body was so still. I watched as the neurologist examined him. There was no movement or response from the middle of his chest down. Ty could barely shrug his shoulders and couldn't move his hands or fingers. The nerves that control breathing in the chest wall and neck had been damaged as well. Fortunately, his diaphragm was unaffected, so he could still breathe on his own without the assistance of a ventilator. I appreciated the importance of that fact, as I knew it would be a significant advantage during his recovery.

Once alone with Ty in his room, I closed my eyes. I said a silent prayer thanking God for His grace in saving the life of this precious young man. With my head bowed, I recall breathing deeply, praying that my son would soon be able to do the same.

A hand gently touched my shoulder. "Dr. Gordon?" As I opened my eyes and turned to the direction of the voice, I heard: "Dr. Gordon, my name is Zaki Ibrahim. I am the surgeon caring for your son."

I didn't know this man from Adam. I didn't know anything about his skill as a surgeon, especially in an urgent circumstance such as this. But shaking his hand and looking deeply into his eyes, I felt comforted immediately. It is said that the eyes are the portals to the soul. This physician's gentle eyes allayed my fears. His gaze silently confirmed to me that everything was in perfect order. It was no coincidence that his path had crossed ours.

He asked if I would like to see the MRI of Tyler's neck. The father in me wanted to say no, but the physician in me couldn't resist. We went into the viewing room, and as I knelt down on one knee next to Dr. Ibrahim, he began scrolling through the various pictures of Tyler's neck. What I saw sent a shiver up and down my spine. It looked as though a bomb had gone off in his neck, with bone fragments everywhere. On the screen, at the site of Tyler's spinal-cord injury, the normally white portion of the spinal cord was speckled with black spots and blotches, the same ones I had seen while looking out the window of the airplane on my way to Denver.

"This is a *very* significant injury, Dr. Gordon," Dr. Ibrahim emphasized, his voice cracking. "As a father myself, I cannot imagine what you're going through. But I will promise you this. I will do my very best to help your son." I was confident that Tyler was in the right hands.

THAT NIGHT WAS THE LONGEST OF MY LIFE. First, they had to operate from the back of his neck. Then they flipped him over and surgically stabilized the front part of his cervical spine. After an eight-hour surgery to decompress Tyler's spinal cord, Dr. Ibrahim emerged from the operating room exhausted. As he took my hand, he drew me into a heartfelt embrace, telling me that the surgery had gone well and Ty would soon be back in the intensive-care unit.

As an invasive cardiologist, after completing a procedure or an operation, I have on many occasions delivered a similar message to family members and friends who were anxiously awaiting my assessment of their loved one's condition. Now being on the receiving end, I can appreciate more fully the impact of those encouraging words. They offered relief of unimaginable proportions. Overcome with emotions, all I could say was, "Thank you, Zaki. Thank you."

I have since learned that *zaki* is Arabic for "bright and pure." The bright and pure spark of the Divine resides in Dr. Zaki Ibrahim. Tyler received the healing energy of the Universe tonight, sculpted through the hands of this gifted surgeon.

Dr. Ibrahim turned and departed. Now alone in the ICU waiting room, I closed my eyes and prayed for my son's healing. This would be the first time I prayed for this. I did not ask for any particular type of healing. I just prayed for healing. It would become the mantra I'd repeat each and every day.

And so our stormy journey began. As I drifted off to sleep that night, my last thought was, *Treat this as if you had chosen it to be. . . .*

THE HAND
THAT ROCKS
THE CRADLE

(July 1st)

Angela arrived in Denver this morning. On the trip from the airport to the hospital, I had the opportunity to prepare her for what she was about to see. Being in the medical field, I was well accustomed to the high-tech equipment required in an intensive-care unit. Angela was not. All of this would be very foreign and frightening to her. I shared with her the purpose of all the various tubes, IVs, and machinery she would see attached to our son. But all of my descriptions couldn't soften the shock she experienced when she first laid eyes on her broken Boosle Boy.

At the doorway, she hesitated, trembling. Taking in what was before her eyes, she gathered her strength, took a deep breath, and entered Tyler's room with a fortitude that literally changed the energy surrounding our son.

Tyler groggily opened his eyes. Relieved that Momma had made it safely, he smiled. Without any words spoken and comforted by her presence, he drifted back off into a deep, deep sleep.

LATER IN THE DAY, Tyler's condition took an abrupt turn for the worse when his respiratory status deteriorated. His breathing became frighteningly labored. The spinal-cord injury had left him scarcely able to clear his throat, much less cough.

The stress on his damaged body resulted in his blood pressure dropping dangerously; his oxygen level plummeted as well. The physician in me kicked in as it had for over a quarter century whenever faced with a similar circumstance of a patient quickly decompensating. In situations such as this, objectivity is of critical importance in being able to make life-and-death decisions unencumbered by emotional interference.

In a nanosecond, I became as focused as a laser beam, able to disconnect from the awareness that this was my son trying to die before my very eyes. Angela ran from the room to find his nurse; none of the doctors were in the intensive-care unit at the time. As the nurse ran back into his room, I shared with her my thoughts as to what might be causing his rapid deterioration and suggested what she should do until Tyler's physician arrived.

Several minutes later, his doctor bolted into the room, thankfully taking control of the situation. I slowly backed away from the bedside; my wife did not. Instead, she gently held Tyler's hand, softly stroking it. The doctor gave some orders, tests were arranged, and measures were instituted to stabilize him.

Angela did not leave his side. It was there she would stay for over an hour until his condition improved.

At one point, while standing in the corner of his room, now a passive observer, I watched for the longest time as Angela's hand gently caressed Ty's. The connection between the two of them is so very strong. In her prayerful vigil, she shared with me, "You know, as I watch Tyler struggle for every breath, it reminds me to breathe myself, to take in prana, the life force of the Universe. I know I should appreciate it all the time, but just now I have become so grateful for each of my breaths. It hurts me so much to watch Tyler so labored in his breathing. It frightens me as I watch his abdomen moving in and out, his opened lips moving slightly as the short, forced puffs of air leave his body. I pray that his next breath will come.

"Terry, my heart overflows with love for this precious young man. I cannot help but smile from the sheer joy of being his momma. I meditate and I pray and I breathe. As I breathe in, I thank God for saving the life of our child." With a serene smile on her face, she adds, "As I breathe out, I am sending all of my energy into Ty. I know my cleansing breath will help our son through this injury."

She closed her eyes, and cradling his hand in hers, she bowed her head ever so slightly in prayer. Her position did not change for hours.

I'LL BE THERE

(July 2nd, 1:00 A.M.)

Exhausted, Angela has drifted off to sleep in the recliner chair in Tyler's room. Our son's condition remains tenuous. It is unnerving for me to watch him as he struggles to clear congestion from his lungs. His cough is virtually nonexistent. The respiratory therapist has shown me how to perform what they call the "quad cough." I place my fist underneath the front of his rib cage, and as he attempts to cough, I forcibly thrust it up into his diaphragm. This is to assist Tyler's weakened coughing mechanism. It seems barbaric, but the nursing staff assures me that it helps in preventing pneumonia from settling in. There are so many things, simple things like a cough, that we take for granted.

How I wish I could trade places with you, son. I wish I could carry your burden, absorb your pain, and assume your fears. I know I cannot do that, but I promise you this, Tyler: I will __always__ be there for you.

Music has forever been important in our lives. When Tyler was a child, I would often play Kenny Loggins's *Return to Pooh Corner* album for him as he drifted off to sleep. I even recall one night while singing along with the album, he begged me, "Dad, stop singing. You're ruining the magic."

Return to Pooh Corner is by far my favorite album of all time. Over the years, whenever I have found myself in the midst of turmoil, I always turn to it to help me reconnect with the innocence of peace. One of my favorite songs on the album is *Cody's Song,* composed by Kenny for his son.

In the quiet of this now silent night, with my son and his momma asleep, I quietly sang *Cody's Song* to him once again. I don't believe my singing ruined the magic for him this time, because I think I saw a little smile appear on his face.

> *When you feel afraid,*
> *When you lose your way, I'll find you,*
> *Just try to smile, and dry your eyes,*
> *I will bring back the moon into your skies.*
> *And ever you will, remember darlin',*
> *I'll be there to:*

Sing to you
I promise you,
I promise to
Comfort you and sing to you
Darlin', I'll be there just for you. . . .

Though you'll grow away
No matter how you'll change
I'll know you.
And when you tire of life alone,
There will always be one sure way back home.

Just turn on the quiet,
And you close your eyes
And listen inside. . . .

I'll be there to sing to you,
I promise you
I promise to
Comfort you
And sing to you.

And darlin', I'll be there,
Anytime, and anywhere,
Darlin', I'll be there just for you.

PART II

THE SKY IS CRYING

GIVE ME THE GOOD NEWS

(July 5th)

In the seven days since Tyler's injury, we have received hundreds of cards, letters, and e-mails, along with many heartfelt prayers from friends, family members, and even total strangers. Until you've had a heart-wrenching experience such as this, it is hard to fathom the power of such loving support. In those moments of solitude when this all seems so overwhelming, the energy from prayers rejuvenates beyond description.

I received something the other day, however, that I must admit took me by surprise. I will preface this by admitting my initial response was a very judgmental one, as I questioned what would possess someone to send something of this nature. Knowing the person as I do, I was certain his intention was not ill willed, just misguided.

He had forwarded to me the link to a newspaper article describing Tyler's automobile accident. Now why would I want to read the graphic account about a horrific accident that nearly killed my son? What would drive me to search the web for a description of anyone's misfortune?

I realized that I was judging not only the sender, but myself as well, because I almost decided to read the article. What was it that drew me to that website? What is it in human nature that draws us to the graphic depictions of tragedies being experienced by others?

A while back, I stopped at a local restaurant for coffee. I smiled as I noticed a father helping his four-year-old son open his Happy Meal. Watching them took me back to a time years ago when Tyler and I would spend quality time with one another; we referred to this special time together as "Men's Club." Seated in the booth of the restaurant, as I was recalling that marvelous experience, I was suddenly yanked into a sad reality.

As the father was taking his son's food out of the bag, I could see that the youngster was not paying attention to the meal or even the toy being placed in front of him. He was mesmerized by the big-screen TV located in the dining area of the restaurant. CNN was showing the vivid images of bloodied, dead college students being carried from the Virginia Tech classrooms, the tragic aftermath of the rampage senselessly inflicted by a crazed young man. I watched this little guy's reaction to what he was watching, and it was obvious by the look on his face that he was horrified.

The irony struck me that this was anything but a happy meal! The sad truth is that in this information age that we live in, it seems that very few of us actually enjoy happy meals, or happy *days* for that matter. As I witnessed that child losing his innocence, it became painfully apparent to me that we have lost balance in our lives.

Many of us seem to thrive on the misfortunes of others. Perhaps this makes us feel more secure because we have as yet escaped such mayhem. I often wonder how many of us honestly feel after watching the news that now bombards us 24/7. What possible good comes from reading a newspaper filled with the tragic events of the day? Do we feel empowered, or are we weakened by constant exposure to such negativity? How many beheadings in Iraq might have been avoided had not the media shown the graphic footage of such atrocities? How many twisted agendas would fail to reach us if we didn't allow ourselves to become poisoned by this constant barrage?

What purpose does the article about Tyler's accident serve? There is nothing any of us can do about it.

What happened has happened. There is no going back. The past cannot be undone. We have chosen as a family not to place any of our thoughts on the accident. There is no blame. Angela described it beautifully: "The hows and whys of yesterday are not important. We will not waste our precious energy revisiting the accident; it is of no significance to us. We love each other very much, and we love Tyler more now than ever before."

For us to heal, there can be no regretted past or agonized future. What is important is that we, together, dedicate ourselves to the only thing we are promised . . . the present moment.

DO YOU BELIEVE IN MAGIC?

(July 8th)

A magical moment occurred this morning. Angela had stayed with Tyler last night, and when I entered the room this morning, she excitedly shared a vivid dream she'd had. In it she kept hearing someone whispering to her, "Magic . . . magic!" This unknown voice even spelled the word out for her, insistent that she be cognizant of the *magic.* She wasn't sure what it meant, but it clearly had gotten her attention.

As gooseflesh appeared on my arms, I shared with my wife a note we received from an acquaintance of Mattie-Rose. It read:

> *Hi Tyler,*
> *My wife and I know Mattie-Rose from our son's kindergarten class where she taught. She*

was extraordinary. And through our attempts to show our gratitude, I exchanged e-mails with your parents, who showed me why she turned out to be so wonderful. You also must have these same qualities. I would bet my life on it.

It goes without saying that this accident has been terribly traumatic for you. But I want to tell you that although it can seem that events are random, every nuance of everything that happens to you or occurs around you has designed purpose and intention. Your response will make all the difference in how your life will be ultimately touched by it.

No matter how hard it might be to feel good about your accident, you must learn to embrace the blessings it can provide. It will be in making yourself feel good about even this that the Universe will be given the signal to pour every possible option into your healing and into you.

The opposite of this approach is, of course, despair and disillusionment. If allowed to overpower you, these will cut off all positive influx of Light and healing.

Be the miracle, Tyler! Assume the winner's confidence that every good and wonderful thing always has and will continue to flow to you with *ease and grace. Your body will obey your mind, as it must. You were never strong because of your bodily attributes; it was always because of your mind.*

As you assure your mom, dad, and family that you will kick even this, they will pick up your confidence and pour even more healing energy into your cells.

If I sound very experienced at this, it's because I am. My little brother, Gerard, also sustained a spinal-cord injury. Since his injury, which was as severe as yours, he has represented the United States in three Olympics in fencing. He plays basketball for the Clippers Big Wheels team and holds numerous medals for skiing and downhill off-road racing.

Now, it took him a little bit of time to get his winning attitude together, but you have the opportunity to pull this together from the get-go. If you can assimilate the right attitude now, you can help your body heal from literally anything! Do the miracle healing now, Tyler. Don't listen to anyone who says you cannot recover from this. Tune it out. Shut it off. Let their reality be theirs, knowing the truth of yours.

I bless you with all the might that the Universe can yield to you. Pray, yes. But know that God gives with ease and grace to those who own it and not necessarily to those who just request it. Make yourself feel what it's like to be healing in record time. Feel this all the time, Tyler, and I'll meet you on the slopes for your next snowboarding trip.

Magic Moreno

What is magic? What is real? Are they actually different? Magic is generally performed by creating an illusion that appears to be unexplainable to the rational mind and its five senses.

For those of us limited by the constraints of the physical world, and who claim that we'll believe it only when we see it, the assumption is that if we are unable to touch, smell, see, taste, or hear something, it must not exist. But consider for a moment all the microscopic organisms that exist. Before the invention of the microscope, the human eye could not visualize them. Did that make them any less real?

We tend to think that only the visible world has reality and structure. The rational mind grounded in the logic of science and physics cannot begin to fathom something magical as anything other than a random occurrence. But the inner world we know as thought, feeling, and imagination may in fact possess structure that is real, one that exists in its own place. The mind, free from the constraints of form, appreciates that indeed there exists another dimension, a higher place from which to draw insight and guidance. This magical space is found in the invisible realm of spirituality. It is from there that we will see it . . . when we believe it.

I found a life changer in *Real Magic,* a book by Dr. Wayne W. Dyer. In it he wrote:

> You have the capacity to create miracles and live a life of real magic, by using your invisible self to influence your physical reality. When you truly become a spiritual being first and a physical being second, and know how to live and breathe in this new alignment, you will become your own miracle worker.

In order to reach the core of the spiritual self, it is important to divert attention away from the superficial material world of form. Surrendering then to the magnetism of this special place, listen to the inner voice that beckons. Once you allow your spiritual eyes to open, heaven will reveal itself, allowing magical and miraculous things to unfold.

We allowed real magic to enter our lives this morning. It appeared in Angela's dream and manifested in the words of Magic Moreno. By including the spiritual dimension of existence, by embracing the power of mind and imagination, a world of miracles will unfold for us. Magical energy is pervasive throughout the cosmos. It is directed by pure love, offering the blessing of Divine guidance.

> *"Miracles are natural. When they*
> *do not occur something has gone wrong."*

> — A Course in Miracles

To Magic Moreno, we thank you. Tyler heard your message; it resonated with him in a marvelous manner. Your *sleight of hand* came to us at just the right moment.

P.S. July 17th, Tyler's birthday, was the very day in 1955 when Disneyland's *Magic* Kingdom first opened its doors. *Hmm . . .*

BEAUTY AND THE BEAST

(July 9th)

As my eyes opened for the first time this morning, the day had already dawned—a beautiful one with the Colorado sun shining brightly into our rented apartment. I paused before arising to allow the beauty of the sun's radiance to bathe me as I spoke the first words of my day: "Thank you. Thank you. Thank you." I felt blessed, so very grateful to God for granting me this day.

Slowly, the reality of our circumstance started to creep its way back into my mind. As it did, I began feeling a sinking sensation, as if I were slowly being swallowed by quicksand. The compressive feeling became stronger with each passing moment. I found myself feeling guilty for enjoying the sunlight when all my son could see was darkness. How selfish of me to enjoy anything when Tyler cannot.

A thought then occurred to me: *Why shouldn't the day be beautiful?* Even though my heart is filled with an indescribable sadness, happiness and beauty needn't be precluded. Why must there be only agony? What would be the purpose of such a limited perspective?

It struck me that the human realm is a perfect circumstance in which to seek transformational enlightenment. All of the pain and turmoil of this existence is perfectly balanced by those things that bring us pleasure as well. An awareness of this apparent dichotomy, that opposites simultaneously exist, allows us to not be overly burdened by the negative aspects of any experience.

A voice silently speaks to me: "Terry, look around you. Can you not see the beauty right before your eyes? It is there right alongside your suffering." For us to survive there must be such equilibrium in our lives, a balance that is manifested by the apparent dualities of life. The hurricane is countered by a calm, sunny day; perfect health is balanced by life-threatening disease or injury; hot by cold; and darkness by illumination. These perceived opposites must be embraced as what they truly are—one and the same. It is the paradox described by Lao-tzu in the second verse of the ancient teachings of the Tao Te Ching:

Under heaven all can see beauty as beauty,
only because there is ugliness.
All can know good as good only because there is evil.

Being and nonbeing produce each other.
The difficult is born in the easy.
Long is defined by short, the high by the low.
Before and after, go along with each other.

So the sage lives openly in apparent duality
and paradoxical unity . . .

And so it is. We must remain grateful for everything that comes our way. Each experience we have places an important tile in the mosaic of life.

REACH THE SUMMIT

(July 11th)

Walking to the grocery store this morning, I noticed a distant mountain range. Although I have looked at these peaks several times before, today there was an allure to them that I found irresistible. There they stood, a majestic background to the Denver skyline, waiting patiently to be noticed by me. They were like a puppy that sits for hours at your side wanting nothing more than just a little bit of your attention.

"Come to me . . . come to me," these mountains beckoned. The attraction to them became so intense that I actually hopped in the car and took off in their direction. Within an hour I reached the place where the flatlands met the foothills. The farther I drove into the soaring peaks, the greater the sense of security I felt; their timeless presence bespoke the wisdom of the ages.

At a rest stop, I pulled over and got out. Leaning against my car, I breathed in this magnificent scenery. The pristine beauty of the Aspen-laced ridges captivated me as they abutted the crystal-blue Colorado sky. Off in the distance, a movement caught my eye. As I focused on it, I could see it was a young man rappelling off the face of a cliff, which had to have been at least a hundred feet or so in height. As I watched his cautious moves, my stomach began to feel queasy as I flashed back to almost 50 years earlier.

I was ten years old at a rustic summer camp in Kentucky called Camp Country Boy, run by Tom Boone, a direct descendant of none other than Daniel Boone. There was this tree house high in an old oak tree. Every kid wanted to be a member of the elite group that spent time in this fortress in the sky. To reach the tree house, you had to first climb an adjacent tree pulling yourself up rung by rung on a rope ladder that dangled from above. Then, in order to cross over to the tree house, you needed to walk on an eight-inch-wide dead tree trunk that had been hoisted up about 30 feet from the ground and laid horizontally between the two trees. As you walked across the 20-foot "gangplank," as it was called, you would hold on to two ropes that were strung between the first and second trees. Stable, it was not!

To become a member of the tribe, you had to negotiate this bridge by yourself. From the get-go, I was absolutely terrified. About halfway across, with all my friends watching, I became paralyzed with fear. I recall this queasy feeling in my gut as I frantically looked back to where I had started. Then, looking forward to where I needed to go, it was apparent that I wasn't going to make it to either side.

Somehow, I ultimately succeeded in crossing the great divide. How I did so, I do not to this day recall. It remains one of those blurs of memory.

Unlike his old man, Tyler has always been fearless. Kahlil Gibran's wisdom rings true to me when he says: "Your children are not your children. . . . They come through you but not from you." Ty's always been a daredevil. Secretly, I have admired that in him. It should come as no surprise that my son is a rock-climbing enthusiast (a sport that I certainly could never embrace).

Prior to today, I had never actually watched anyone rock climb. I must admit that I gained a new perspective watching this man adeptly negotiate the face of that chiseled mountain. For the first time, I let go and allowed myself to imagine the exhilaration Tyler must experience as he engages in this vertical game of chess.

I let myself imagine what must go through his mind as he dangles precariously from a few ropes and hooks hundreds of feet above a canyon floor. I envision Tyler's rock-hard, chiseled body exploring the contour of the surface of the cliff as he twists and adjusts his stance to find just the right position. Only then does he commit himself, melding with the jagged edge of the precipice. My mind watches as he feels the rock's surface much like a blind person reads Braille and slips his agile fingers into its small crevasses. Then contracting every muscle with all his might, he locks his entire body into place. Drawing himself into a tight embrace with the rock face, the mountain and the man become one.

Envisioning this precision dance in a new light, I could appreciate how demanding the sport must be, challenging a person both physically and mentally. Rock climbing tests not only the climber's strength and agility, but his endurance as well. Once you begin, you can't very well quit in the middle of a climb or, as I reflected, in between two trees.

The metaphor is intriguing. When faced with an overwhelming obstacle, doubt may enter the mind, replacing confidence. Fear takes control. The ensuing suffering can itself be paralyzing. Changed by a transforming event, Tyler is now engaged in the climb of his life. Of course he is discouraged by the loss of independence, now having to rely on others for his most basic needs. It is easy to understand the indignity of his predicament as he mourns the forfeiture of control over his life. His greatest fear is of the loss of what he had most relied upon throughout his life to define who he was: his body. One can only imagine how terrifying it must be to realize that life as you knew it has disappeared.

No doubt the loneliness created by these fears is having a crippling effect on him. Part of this loneliness is from the fear of losing himself. Similar feelings might arise from being separated from those things in life that have provided superficial pleasure, a false sense of identity or self-worth. This could occur with the loss of one's job, the ending of a relationship, a precipitous drop in the value of one's financial portfolio, or, in Tyler's case, the demise of his autonomy.

Regardless of what's lost, the response is generally the same—to react out of fear. This has an insidious way of affecting every other aspect of our existence. Ultimately, this can negatively shape our attitude and approach to the life that remains. Doors of opportunity slam shut, preventing us from handling whatever challenges lie before us. In this frame of mind, it becomes extremely difficult to be receptive to the beauty that still abounds right alongside the perceived misery.

What is left for us to then attract into our lives is the very thing we had hoped to avoid—the darkness.

If, however, you do not allow fear to gain entry into your consciousness, the limitations imposed by this worldly existence cannot encumber you. Through knowing yourself to be a spiritual being having only a temporary human experience, this life can be experienced as a passive observer, that as Lao-tzu described, can "witness the end without ending." No longer will you be encumbered or incapacitated by your own fears. You will be empowered to continue the climb.

I see my son scrambling up the sheer rock face of his life, scratching and scraping the surface as he moves along. He may take some missteps that humble him; adjustments will have to be made. All the while, I applaud the fortitude of this young man. I watch as the small but significant strides he makes inch him upward toward his goal. He may occasionally lose his footing; pebbles may tumble and fall from beneath his feet. There will likely be days when he relinquishes ground, enduring times when hope might be lost. But ultimately, I see Tyler reaching the summit, successfully conquering his own Mount Everest.

HERE COMES THE SUN

(July 12th)

This Sunday morning was anything but a *sun* day. The Denver skies were gray, overcast, and heavy. A big storm was rapidly approaching, a gloomy beginning for day 13 of our new journey.

Sitting on the grass, I contemplated the sun, this ancient luminous star at the center of our solar system. Having formed over 4.5 billion years ago, it continues selflessly to provide warmth and light to our Earth. It supports all life, transforming everything it reaches. I am graced to receive its abundant energy. Yet as I settled deeper into my meditative state, I felt the need to reciprocate by directing my energy back toward the sun, thanking it for the blessings of its nurturing radiance. I marveled that despite the fact that the sun hangs in the Universe more than 93 million miles away, its beneficial rays reached me in only about 8 minutes and 19 seconds!

The sun has always intrigued humanity. It has been regarded by many cultures as a deity, a god whose presence rising above the horizon creates the day and whose absence when it falls below the horizon yields the night. Ancient cultures like the Incas and Aztecs constructed mammoth monuments dedicated to the sun. Even the word *Sunday* comes from reverence to this bright star in the sky.

So on this Sunday . . . where *was* the sun? Even in the midst of the ever-darkening skies, I knew that it was shining somewhere not too far away. Despite the feeling that life may appear at this moment to be at a standstill, it is, after all, the nature of the Universe to remain in perpetual motion. While we may find our inner light temporarily obscured by the cloud coverage, it is never extinguished.

As I meditated, I re-created this cloudy, gloomy day anew with the sun peaking its head above the Colorado mountains bidding all a good morning. Imagine that, re-creating the day in your mind! By changing your thoughts and deciding ahead of time what your day will be like, you can actually impact the experience you are about to have. As my meditation expanded, the sun rose in the sky. It felt like the exhilarating moment when a jetliner, surrounded by the thickness of gray clouds, suddenly eclipses the top edge of the cloud coverage and bursts into the blue above. I somehow knew that on this day the sun would play a pivotal role in the lives of those in the Gordon family.

As the day progressed, Tyler was pensive and made little eye contact. I could tell where his thoughts had taken him. He made several comments that indicated he was digging an ever-deepening hole for himself. When I opened the curtains in his room, he asked me to shut them. He had no interest in seeing the light.

A bed at Craig Hospital, where they specialize in taking care of patients with spinal-cord injuries, had not yet become available to him, and we all had been anticipating a bright change of scenery. But Ty's reaction to the news was: "It won't make a difference anyway."

I replied, "You know, son, you're absolutely right. It won't make any difference." That got his attention. He looked over at me like I was crazy. "Until you decide to change the thought, you won't get any better. It's not going to matter where you are, whether it is in this hospital or over at Craig Hospital, in Durango or at home in Ohio. All of the marvelous healing energy being extended on your behalf, this incredible flow being sent your way, is being deflected from you by the bunker you have built around yourself." I suggested, "Let the sun shine in, Ty! You'll feel so much better." He remained silent, turning his head away from me.

Cloudy days are important in the overall scheme of things. It is very difficult to fully appreciate the beauty of sunlight until you know what it's like to be without it. Several hours later, I was walking outside when the sun began breaking through the cloud cover. Everything touched by its brilliant rays seemed to come alive. Watching the light spreading across the distant mountain range, I realized I was looking at the same glorious reflection that years ago inspired John Denver to write the song "Sunshine on My Shoulders."

Upon my return to his room, humming that tune, I noticed the sun peeking its way through Tyler's partially closed curtain. It gently caressed a flowered plant, whose brilliant colors awakened, filling his entire room with a vibrant luminescence. The Universe had delivered the eternal message of sunlight. Life is destined to continue.

Several minutes later, Tyler posed a question to me that brought tears to my eyes: "Pops, do you think I could go outside to be in the sunshine?"

We spent over 30 glorious minutes outside bathing in the radiant, nurturing warmth of the late-afternoon sun. It reminded me of a quote from an ancient Tibetan saint: "When the sun of fierce devotion shines on the snow mountain of the master, the stream of his blessings will pour down."

HEY GOD, WHERE ARE YOU?

(July 15th)

During times of trouble when adversity strikes in overwhelming fashion, our fortitude may begin to waver. Despair causes us to question how a good God could sit back and let bad things happen to us. Many give up on God when their prayers go unanswered, crying out, "Hey God, where are You?"

Despite the grave circumstance in which we now find ourselves, I remain steadfast that the Author of Life hasn't abandoned us. He is involved in everything that happens—whether it is perceived as good or bad.

He reminded me of that today with a wink. Both Angela and I have the appreciation that *all* things are possible. As a physician, I can tell you that doctors don't know everything . . . we just think we do!

As I was contemplating the possibility of Tyler fully recovering from his injury, the scientist in me had to accept that the statistical probability of that happening was low. It was then that I remembered one of my patients, Mike Petras. He had been a heart patient of mine for many years, and during that time we had developed a friendship that extended well beyond the patient-doctor relationship.

About four years ago, he was diagnosed with stage III pancreatic cancer. He was told to quickly get his affairs in order, as he had mere months to live. As a last-ditch effort, a surgeon attempted an operation to remove the cancerous tumor, only to abort the procedure once he opened Mike up. What he found was that the cancer was far too advanced; the risk of surgery far outweighed the minimal benefit it could offer. My friend was sent home to die.

With prayer, along with chemotherapy and radiation therapy, Mike surprised everyone. Despite the odds, he has survived. His last CAT scan showed no evidence of tumor—none!

As a member of the scientific community, statistics are generally how we quantify and justify our evidence-based approach to medicine. Certainly, the statistical probability of Mike surviving not only months but now for four years is less than 2 percent. As Vin Scully supposedly once said: "Statistics are used much like a drunk uses a lamppost: for support, not illumination."

Could Mike's good health be the result of a miracle? I believe so.

THIS MORNING THERE WAS A SINGLE voice-mail message on my cell phone. "Hi, if this is the former cardiologist Dr. Terry Gordon, please give me a call. It's your friend Mike Petras."

I called him right back. He had heard of our misfortune and wanted to share with me that his thoughts and prayers were with Tyler and us. I shared with Mike my recent thoughts about his "incurable" disease and how he had crossed my mind while I was contemplating the possibility of a miracle for our son. Mike informed me that he continues to do well and let me know that my name had come up recently.

I have been involved in national legislation, the Josh Miller HEARTS Act, a bill that will place automated external defibrillators (AEDs) in every school in the U.S. It is currently working its way through the U. S. Senate. One of the cosponsors is Senator Sherrod Brown of Ohio. I had actually just placed a call to his office last week, but had yet to hear back.

Mike went on to tell me that his daughter, who works for Sherrod Brown in D.C., is involved in the bill and was wondering about this cardiologist from Akron who was spearheading the initiative. He excitedly shared with his daughter that her dad's cardiologist was the same man! Moi!

What I have discovered in my life is that synchronicity is no coincidence. Connectivity such as this remains an affirmation to me that the Divine is indeed intricately involved in what we do. So during times of trouble, when I may I pose the question, "Hey God, where are You?" I am not surprised by the response, "Why, I am in front of you, I am behind you. I am standing to your right and beside you on your left. I am below you, and I am also above you. Where else could I be?"

A SONG OF BIRTH

(July 17th)

Twenty-two years ago, Angela suffered a miscarriage. We had been blessed with three healthy daughters, and we both knew that whatever was to be would be. Besides, I definitely had the mojo back then. I'm not bragging, but I could look at Angela and she would get pregnant! Okay, I *am* bragging.

So, within two months of the miscarriage we were once again blessed with child, and the pregnancy was progressing well. In fact, Angela looked like she was carrying quintuplets, not that she was fat. . . .

At the age of 34 and with the recent miscarriage, it was suggested that Angela undergo an amniocentesis to make sure that everything was okay. The following week she underwent the procedure. Complications occurred as the physician stuck a needle into her abdomen, which resulted in the loss of all the fluid from her amniotic sac. She was rushed to the hospital, where the physicians shared with us that in all likelihood we would lose our baby.

Angela was placed on bed rest with the head of the bed angled downward to take the pressure off her uterus. The doctors warned us of infection, damage to the fetus, and even the significant risk to Angela's life if we didn't terminate the pregnancy.

One night after tucking our three daughters into bed, I called Angela at the hospital. It was around 2:00 A.M., and it had been a sleepless night for both of us. We talked about the consensus of opinion from her physicians that we should abort the pregnancy. As a rule, I had been the one in our family to make medical decisions, and I told her that we should trust the recommendation of our physicians.

Angela shared that she could feel our baby fighting inside her, and she simply could not abandon it. She *knew* that everything would be okay. Now, my wife has had these knowings before. And I must admit that she had usually been right on. Accepting that our baby could have serious problems, I deferred to her maternal instinct for guidance. I knew that we had the strength to handle whatever would come our way.

Gradually, the amniotic fluid began recollecting, and serial ultrasounds indicated an apparently healthy fetus. The remainder of the pregnancy was uneventful. In the late afternoon on July 17th, 1988, our son, Tyler Albert Gordon, joined us in this world. The delivery was complicated. The umbilical cord had wrapped itself in two true knots around his neck, and even one could have strangled him to death during the delivery. When the doctor told Angela this, she just smiled. You see, she knew Tyler was meant to survive. He was coming into this world with his own dharma, his unique purpose.

Birth is an interesting concept. Most of us consider the day we were born as our birthday. In truth, we existed long before the day we vigorously emerged from the comfort of our mother's womb. Science has confirmed that at the precise moment of what we generally define as conception, something already exists. From each contributor to fertilization, the DNA information coalesces to orchestrate a miraculous process that results in a human being with uniqueness never before manifested.

Contrary to common belief, birth is not a creation from nothingness. Before life becomes life, there is life-consciousness. Rather than an abrupt start to life with our first breath, birth is more of a continuation of the life force that forever has been and forever will be. The flow of this vital force is the same for all things; no difference exists between the flow of life force in Tyler Gordon's blood vessels and the flow of melting snow as it thaws and becomes a trickling mountain stream that gradually builds up speed and power and eventually empties into a magnificent waterfall. The flow of nature's energy in all things promotes the very momentum that guarantees survival, ensuring its existence for eternity.

This day is the 21st year we have celebrated the continuation of Tyler's flow of life force now in physical form. We requested kindred spirits to join us in petitioning the Universe on Tyler's behalf by sending prayers and energy his way at precisely 7:17 this morning. We received an especially poignant message sent by a friend. The words of Marie-Josee Dubois eloquently expressed the intimate nature of the Universe: "Que ce jour du 17 juillet resplendisse de toutes les graces divines et de joie profonde, provenant de cette communion de prieres et de tout cet amour reunis." Translated, it means, "This day of July 17 is resplendent with all the divine graces and joy coming from this communion of conjoined prayers and love."

Today, we palpably felt the vibrant life force from each of you, our loved ones. With gratitude in our hearts, we basked in the energy directed our way, the synergy of kindred spirits empowering us beyond imagination.

Albert Einstein once wrote:

> A human being is a part of the whole, called by us the "Universe," a part limited in time and space. He experiences himself, his thoughts and feelings as something separated from the rest—a kind of optical illusion of his consciousness. This delusion is a kind of prison for us, restricting us to our personal desires and to affection for a few persons nearest us. Our task must be to free ourselves from the prison by widening our circle of compassion to embrace all living creatures and the whole of nature in its beauty.

Tyler's injury has been the catalyst for us to connect with many people around the world, some of whom we have never met. The prayers offered for him demonstrate love in its most distilled form. It is from this consciousness that we learn to "love thy neighbor as thyself," not just because it's a nice thing to do, but because thy neighbor *is* thyself, despite living half a world away.

Humanity is like the vast ocean. At its deepest spot, the ocean is uniform, similar in its makeup, consistent in its calmness. But as one peers at the ocean's windswept surface, many waves can be seen. Some are very large, others quite small. Although each one may appear to be separate, in truth there is no individuation. After all, a wave is nothing more than the ocean pushing up on itself. There is no demarcation between the whitecap of a wave on the surface and the deepest part of the ocean; they are one in the same, never disconnected. The ocean and the wave are both water; they differ only in form.

We, too, are all connected—conjoined as one, inseparably linked to our common Source. When we come to appreciate that the suffering of each person in this world is *our* suffering, each child dying of starvation in Darfur is *our* child dying, each death of a protester for freedom is *our* death, and each young man's spinal-cord injury is *our* injury, it is only then that we become whole.

On this special day, July 17th, 2009, many of us conjoined with one another. We gave of ourselves, sending healing energy laced with unconditional love to one beautiful soul.

THE RAIN
DON'T LAST

(July 21st)

Yesterday proved emotionally difficult for Tyler. His birthday celebration from four days ago had lost its luster. The helium balloons that once danced around the ceiling of his room were now beginning to wilt, collapsing back into themselves. Tyler's sisters Laila and Britt left Denver and returned to their lives. Britt flew back to Durango, Laila and Angela to Richfield. (Angela needed to see her doctor and would return to Denver in a couple of days.) Mattie-Rose will delay her return to Ohio for another few days. She and I will attempt to fill the void left by Tyler's departing loved ones.

Last night, alone with Ty in his room, I helped him with a late-night snack. He was very pensive. Sadness exuded from him like a weeping wound. It was one of those rare moments when he opened up to me, sharing his deepest feelings of dark despair.

I must constantly remind myself of his view of the world. His perspective is from lying in a bed in the same 10' x 10' hospital room day after day after day. In his weakened condition, he must rely on others to help him when he wishes to change position in bed. Only then can he look in a different direction and perhaps adjust his view of the world. While Angela has added her special touches to his otherwise gloomy room, this sterile environment is his universe. He cannot see out the window. If he could, all he would see are the bricks and mortar of a nearby adjacent building. Indeed, his world is much contracted.

The bed at Craig Hospital will become available in several days, which is none too soon. We all need a change of scenery. The rehabilitation potential for Tyler is infinite. I just wish I knew how to convince him to embrace that thought.

Tonight, he shared with me the ocean of suffering he is enduring with the indignity of relying on others to perform even his most basic needs. He conveyed the sadness he felt for the impact this ordeal has had on our family. He apologized for "ruining" our lives.

For a long time, there was silence as both of us contemplated his words. My response to him was simply:

"Son, even God doesn't create a storm that lasts forever. We must be patient, Ty. The sun *will* rise again. I promise you."

Shortly thereafter, we both drifted off to sleep.

Forty-five minutes later, a nurse barged in, frantically yanking Ty's curtains closed. The National Weather Service had just issued a tornado warning for our area. As a precautionary measure, Tyler's bed was quickly moved away from the window to the other side of the room.

As we watched The Weather Channel, the Doppler radar graphically showed the strong front moving in our direction; in fact, the heart of the front was aimed directly at us. The thunderous storm dropped two inches of rain in less than 30 minutes. It also brought with it powerful winds of 80 miles per hour and golf ball–sized hail. Fierce bolts of lightning illuminated the nighttime sky as the hospital lights flickered and the emergency-generator system kicked on. We could hear the wind gusting outside our window, feeling the strength of the storm as the windowpane quivered against this awesome power of nature.

And then, as suddenly as danger had approached, things calmed down. The violent turbulence of the storm was replaced by quiet serenity. As the rainstorm lost its strength and the winds gently died down, the

Doppler radar returned to normal. Tyler looked over at me and smiled. He had gotten the message. *No storm lasts forever.*

REJUVENATION

(July 25th)

I arrived at the hospital early this morning before any of the patients were awake. Slowly, I walked along the dimly lit corridors. Outside each room was a wheelchair. Each one had a patient's last name on it, having been customized for that person's particular needs. The wheelchairs' batteries were plugged into the electrical sockets being recharged. Rejuvenating energy trickled its way into each, encouraging its cells back to life.

Passing each room, I peered inside. In the darkness, I could see the outlines of patients lying in bed, their "battery packs" being recharged as well. For most, slumber can be a rejuvenating respite. For others, sleep serves as a means for escape, the wish being to just close your eyes and either awaken to find that the whole ordeal has been but a terrible dream or . . . not to awaken at all.

Ninety patients are still fast asleep this dawn, some with a family member sleeping nearby on a couch or reclining chair. Spinal-cord injuries know no age or racial boundary; there is no gender or socioeconomic discrimination. There are no specific religious or spiritual requirements. The causes of the injuries vary. Many are sporting accidents; others are car or motorcycle mishaps. There was one individual who had tripped at home over his kitten. His fall resulted in a cervical spinal-cord injury that left him paralyzed. Patients come from all walks of life. There are people of all shapes and sizes. It is a diverse mix of humanity. There is no special treatment; every individual is special in the eyes of this marvelously gifted staff.

Each person is at a different stage of healing and recovery, each battery at a different phase of rejuvenation. Some are fully charged, quite energetic, positive in their outlook, and proactive in their approach to rehabilitation. Others with their batteries partially depleted have yet to fully embrace the healing process and sluggishly go through the motions of physical therapy. Sadly, a few whose batteries seem to be totally depleted may not choose the restorative process at all. You can see it in their eyes. These patients view their injury as a death sentence.

Most of us consider death in relation to our definition of life. But conceptually, it encompasses more than just the extinction of life as we know it in the physical sense. The death of one's legs or arms, hands or fingers, or even way of life can be equally as devastating.

Years ago, while at Emory University studying for my B.A. in psychology, I read *On Death and Dying* by Elisabeth Kübler-Ross, M.D. She described in great detail the five stages an individual generally goes through during the process of physically dying. It struck me that with the death of any facet of one's life, the same five stages would likely be experienced.

The first phase Kübler-Ross explained is *denial* and *isolation.* Unconsciously, we all consider ourselves indestructible—as if we're Evel Knievel. Thus, it might become extremely difficult to admit the reality of a devastating accident that denies us our invincibility.

The second stage, *anger,* replaces the denial stage and includes rage, resentment, and even envy. The anger may be directed toward God, medical personnel, or displaced onto family members or friends.

Stage three involves *bargaining,* trying to work out a deal with God. An example might be trying to negotiate an agreement, such as, "If God will heal me, I'll promise to dedicate the remainder of my life to Him."

The fourth heralds *depression.* As one realizes the loss, be it health or the loss of autonomy and familiar surroundings, feelings of sadness and despair take over.

Acceptance is the final stage. If one can work through the preceding phases, a place of peace can be reached where one is neither depressed nor angry about his fate, able to then move on.

I am observing Tyler as he weaves in and out of several of these stages. I also know that we as family members will likely go through similar emotions and sentiments as well. The length of time each of us spends in a particular phase will depend upon our individual needs. It will also be dependent on where we were spiritually when we first embarked on this new leg of our individual journey.

For me personally, the denial stage lasted about 20 seconds. My training as a physician robbed me of this initial step. My education and understanding of medicine, anatomy, and neurology allowed me to immediately grasp the magnitude of our son's injury. For others in the family, perhaps Tyler included, denial will continue until its time is up.

As I entered his room this morning, Ty remained in that faraway place of peaceful slumber, his respite from the nightmare. There is something so genuinely innocent about a sleeping person. I sat next to him in the darkness with my hand gently placed on his, acknowledging that he is using sleep to escape.

I know there are those patients whose batteries are so depleted that they just cannot hold a charge any longer. They are done. There are others, like my son, who have but temporarily lost their connection with the Source of energy. I pray that he will soon choose to reattach his jumper cables to the battery charger and, rejuvenated, decide to forge ahead.

AN ANGEL PASSING THROUGH MY ROOM

(July 26th)

For as long as I have known her, Angela has invoked the angels to assist her in times of need. In the past, I have made fun both of her and her "celestial messengers," as she refers to them. But my wife has always remained steadfast in her belief that in order to receive their guidance, one must not only believe in the angels, but be receptive to them as well. The Greek word *Angelos* means messenger, and she explains that angels function as emissaries, envoys who connect the material world with the spiritual realm.

I have often wondered if these beings really exist. After all, the major religions say they do, and each one has some involvement with angels:

- Gabriel appeared to Mary at Nazareth and to Mohammed at Mecca.

- An angel visited Abraham, who was then convinced not to sacrifice his son Isaac.

- Angels announced the resurrection of Christ.

- The angel Moroni gave the golden plates of the Church of Jesus Christ of Latter-Day Saints to Joseph Smith.

- The Catholic catechism teaches that the existence of angels is a "truth of faith."

- Every Catholic Mass is an act of praise. Worshippers join their voices with the angelic choirs.

- The Second Coming is to be featured by angels.

Polls show that 75 percent of Americans believe in angels. Who am I, then, to disagree with the majority— or for that matter, the angel in my life, my wife?

Several nights ago, Angela was alone with Tyler in his hospital room. She observed a flurry of energy whisk past her, swirling around the room and then gently settling on Tyler. As she told me later, "Feeling a sense of gratitude at its presence, I walked to the other side of Tyler's bed. There was a blue light, an aura surrounding Tyler's head. Then, Divine white light that was centered above his head slowly moved down through his body. As I stepped back, I could see standing before us a tall, radiant angel with masculine energy. Almost reaching the ceiling, the angel had a deep pink robe, bright reddish-orange hair, a halo glow of pale orange, and large golden wings that wrapped around Ty's hospital bed. There was a single tear in the corner of the angel's eyes. His obvious love for our son and the protection he brought him gave me profound peace.

The days that have followed find Tyler's angel standing guard beside him in silent vigil as he cradles him in pure love. I am reassured of God's protective presence.

TODAY HAS BEEN A ROUGH ONE FOR TY. He has been filled with sadness and hopelessness. Despite our attempts to bolster him, he's remained in deep despair. As I left his room to go to the nurses' station, I noticed a man standing outside Tyler's room. I smiled at him and went on my way. When I returned ten minutes later, he was still in the same place, hesitantly peering through the crack in the partially closed door. I asked if I could be of assistance. His almost apologetic and humble reply was that he was one of Tyler's professors from Durango and wanted to stop by for a moment to give him a boost. I had the distinct feeling that this kind gentleman would have stayed out in the hall for hours until he felt the time was right to enter the room.

I invited Dr. Cameron Cooper into Ty's room, and he told us a miraculous story. His life was going smoothly until he received the shock of his life: he was diagnosed with a very large brain tumor. He described to Tyler the courage and fortitude he found deep within himself to battle the disease that doctors said would likely end his life. Despite the tumor, the poor prognosis offered by his physicians, and the terrible side effects he endured from radiation and chemotherapy, Dr. Cooper never missed one day of work *and* completed his Ph.D.

Timing is everything! His math instructor's story noticeably touched Tyler; I could see it in his eyes. I could sense he was rethinking the negative thoughts he was having the moment before Dr. Cameron Cooper entered our room and our lives.

I am sending an angel before you, to keep you safe on the way. Pay attention to him and heed his voice . . .

— Exodus **23:20–21**

Angela and I had been struggling all day to find a way to help pull our son from of the quagmire of his misery. But then an angel arrived at our door. He had driven five hours from Durango just to be with Tyler. While he could have made better time had he used his wings, this angel touched down right on time.

I'M GOIN' HOME

(July 30th)

Yesterday was very difficult. I left Tyler for first time in over four weeks. I was hesitant to leave him, but had to make the trip back to Ohio to take care of a few household details. I was sad beyond imagination, but I knew he would be in good hands with his momma.

The flight home was a melancholy one. I looked forward to seeing Laila and Mattie-Rose, along with Kavenna, our "grand puppy." Mattie-Rose picked me up at the airport. On the ride home, though, I grew more and more apprehensive. I hadn't thought much about home the whole month I'd been in Denver.

Pulling into our driveway was surreal. As we approached the house, I suddenly felt as if I were a stranger to the place we've called home for the last 15 years. When I walked inside, I was greeted by endless licks all over my face by Kavenna. While I appreciated his exuberant greeting, my mind was elsewhere. Aimlessly, I walked through the house just looking around. I was in a fog. Everything seemed sadly foreign to me. It was as if I had been in prison for 30 years and was now returning to a world where time had stood still.

In his book *Man's Search for Meaning,* Viktor Frankl described the agonizing years he spent in a concentration camp in Nazi Germany. When he and his fellow prisoners were finally set free, they all expected to be ecstatically joyous. It turned out to be quite the opposite. He wrote: "'Freedom'—we repeated to ourselves, and yet we could not grasp it. We had said this word so often during all the years we dreamed about it, that it had lost its meaning. Its reality did not penetrate into our consciousness. . . . We came to meadows full of flowers. We saw and realized that they were there, but we had no feelings about them. . . ."

Just as a survivor of Auschwitz, I found myself in a world where I did not feel like I belonged. As I wandered through our house, I noticed Tyler's guitar in the living room leaning against the sofa. It remained in the same spot where he had left it on his last visit home.

I took note of the things I had left as I rushed from our home that chaotic morning more than a month ago. Those things, too, had remained untouched. Frozen in time, they waited patiently for my return to finish tasks left undone.

As I looked around, the feelings of that dreadful morning slowly reemerged. I stepped outdoors and sat on a bench overlooking our lake. The sun had already set, and a low mist had descended. I could barely see the white swans on the other side where they had bedded down for the night. The outline of the treetops marked a distinct line between the majestic forest and the ever-darkening gray skies. Sadness and despair completely filled my soul as I sat there alone, sobbing quietly.

I looked out at the beauty, at the swans and the lake, and allowed myself to think about all of the beloved outdoor activities that Tyler would so terribly miss. He cherished walking in the woods, fishing in the lake, and working on cars in the barn. How could he ever accept his lot? How could he ever heal from this pain?

It was then that I recalled something Angela and I had discussed many years ago when dreaming about our future as retirees. We call our home and the breathtaking surrounding landscape Chestnut Hills. It is truly a piece of heaven. We have been blessed as temporary stewards of this pristine place of peace. Our dream had been to turn Chestnut Hills into a center where those in need could come and begin the healing process in a nurturing environment.

As I sat there on the bench with the evening in its infancy, the veil of sadness started to lift from me, lightening my heart. The words of the Divine came to me once again: "Treat this as if it was something you had chosen." I smiled as I realized that God had just reminded me once again that everything *is* in perfect order. Our healing center, the idea of which was born over a decade ago, will finally come to fruition. Soon Chestnut Hills will welcome its first participant, providing its special healing energy to him. That extraordinary recipient, of course, will be our son.

Goethe once said, "He is the happiest, be he king or peasant, who finds peace in his home." I was home . . . and it was good.

YOU'LL NEVER WALK ALONE

(August 1st)

I awoke early this morning and stepped outside into nature's wonderland. The sun rose over the treetops of Chestnut Hills. A light fog remained draped over our lake, waiting for the warmth of the sun to begin melting it away. A lone blue heron stood as still as still could be. He balanced on one leg, patiently awaiting his first meal of the day.

I marveled at how this prehistoric-looking bird could remain so focused, balancing on a leg that appeared to bend in the wrong direction. What practice it must take; what patience he must have. Most of the time, the heron soars solo in search of food. It is a lonely quest, but one this animal accepts as being in the natural order of things.

Watching this marvelous creature, I pondered my own balancing act. Lately, maintaining equilibrium in my life has proven extremely difficult.

Most of us surround ourselves with loved ones who support us in times of need. But our journey at its most basic level is much like that of the blue heron—a solitary one. Anyone dealing with a terrible disease, disability, or loss no doubt feels a sense of isolation and abandonment. Every time I hear of a suicide, my first thought is of the utter loneliness that person must have felt when considering death as a possible solution to suffering. How sad to contemplate this alone, and even more so to think of acting on it with no one there to hold his or her hand at the final moment.

What is often forgotten amidst the pain and suffering is that we are never, ever alone. We are neither separated, nor separate, from God. Each living being is an inextricably connected part of the Divine. Our spirit, the energy from which we come, is of that Source. Just like the blue heron, we human beings are of God. With that spirit residing within, how could one ever be alone?

In awe, I watched this bird for well over an hour this morning. Balancing on one leg, he never moved a muscle. I wondered what would happen if that leg were injured. The loss of one leg, much less both, would throw everything out of balance for him. He would likely not survive for long.

The blue heron suddenly jabbed at the surface, catching a small fish, which he quickly swallowed whole. In an instant, he lifted off in graceful flight, landing high in the trees.

Driving to Namaste Yoga for my class, thoughts of Ty and the blue heron crossed my mind. As I entered the studio, I felt guilt ridden. I was able to walk into the studio, and for now my son cannot. I felt sad that I was embracing life while my son could not.

The practice of yoga is self-actualizing. It matters not what poses someone beside you can or cannot do. What is important is that you stay focused on your own movements, concentrating on your balance. Today, I dedicated my yoga practice to Ty. I strove to be like the blue heron, in perfect balance, but since I had not been to a yoga class in more than two months, my movements were a little rusty.

Our instructor, Mary Pat Murphy, asked us to attempt triangle pose, which involves a difficult balance. I could not do it. Then she paired us up. With the assistance of a partner, I was able to easily strike the pose and maintain it with relative ease. With a little help from my friend, I achieved perfect balance.

As I held the pose, the chi was flowing. Thoughts of Tyler flooded my mind. In the practice of yoga, one can direct healing breath to a particular joint or muscle for relief. Just as effectively, energy can be channeled to the broken places in our lives, promoting healing at the spiritual level. We can also share this gift with others, directing our energy to their broken places.

I cannot wait to return to my son's side. I ask God to grant me the strength to help support him, to lift him up and assist him in whatever poses in life he chooses.

BUT FOR THE GRACE OF GOD

(August 4th)

I arrived back in Denver last night. This morning, I awoke with renewed energy. By 8:00 A.M. I was in Ty's room watching him sleep. He and Angela had made me a sign: "Ter/Pops, Welcome back to Denver. We missed you (well, not in the A.M.)!" I took the hint.

I am the Lone Ranger of the family when it comes to early-morning rising and shining. When I realized that Ty wasn't going to join me in waking up at this hour, I left to take care of some business. After photo-copying several documents, I rushed out of the hospital and headed to the FedEx office.

I began walking briskly in the direction of my car. A little old lady was shuffling at a snail's pace on the sidewalk in my path. She was at least 80 years old and hunched over as she walked. Her chin was frozen in a severe flexed position that allowed her to see only by lifting her eyes to the top of her eye sockets. Six plastic bags full of groceries weighed her down. She had already shuffled for more than three blocks from the local grocery store, and the bags appeared to be very cumbersome.

She wore tattered, threadbare clothing and a fishing hat over her gray hair to protect her eyes from the glare of the early Denver sun. I whisked past her on my mission to get to FedEx and back before Tyler awakened.

I got to my car, turned on the ignition, and cranked up the air conditioner . . . when I was struck by a thought: *I don't really have it that bad. I'm able to walk to my car without difficulty. I'm sitting in an air-conditioned vehicle, protected from the heat. I'm able to go anywhere I wish in safety and comfort. I have plenty of food and clothing.* And then it hit me that I had just thoughtlessly blasted past an unfortunate elderly woman who would struggle for God knows how many more blocks in the 85-degree weather, carrying her bags back home.

I put the car in gear and turned in the opposite direction of FedEx. I drove back to the spot where I had last seen her, but she was gone. I drove around for a few minutes until I found her walking up a rather steep hill on one of the side streets. Her movements were decidedly more sluggish now. I pulled the car up to her and got out, approaching her from behind.

"Excuse me, ma'am. Ma'am, may I help you?" I asked.

She slowly turned around and with a broad, almost toothless smile, she musically responded, "Oh, no. I'm doing just fine! But thank you, sir, for your kind offer."

She had the most beautiful hazel eyes I have ever seen; I became mesmerized by her gaze. As we looked into each others' eyes, I felt an immediate connection. Her entire essence smiled through those eyes, her radiance revealing to me a beautiful soul. She added, "God bless you, child."

I turned to walk away. Taking a few steps, I paused and looked back at her and smiled. She had resumed her journey, shuffling along the pavement. It amazed me that I had come upon a person for whom I had been feeling sympathy and sorrow. And *she* was blessing *me*. I was envious, wanting to own the peace and fortitude of this woman. She could have very easily accepted my offer of assistance and ridden in the comfort of my air-conditioned car for the duration of her trip back home. Instead, she chose to continue along her path, arduous as it was.

As I watched her walk away, the proverb, "But for the grace of God go I," scrolled through my mind. I was thinking that were it not for God's grace, it could be me carrying those cumbersome bags of groceries, struggling to walk uphill on this humid day. Then the strangest thing happened. As she walked away, I could have sworn I heard her say, "But for the grace of God go I."

"The dying, the crippled, the mentally ill, the unwanted, the unloved—they are Jesus in disguise."

— MOTHER TERESA

HIDING UNDERWATER

Yesterday morning I walked past one of the beautiful parks on the Craig Hospital property. I took a detour off my usual path and entered the park to savor its beauty for a few moments. I noticed a man seated in a fully electric wheelchair. He had parked himself over in the corner of a sitting area with his back as close as possible to the foliage. He almost appeared hunkered down. His shoulders were rounded forward and slumped, and he had a dejected look on his face. I smiled a good morning to him, but his response was anemic at best.

As I continued, I noticed another wheelchair-bound gentleman who was probably in his 50s. He was using a spring-loaded device attached to a fishing pole that enabled him to cast a line. With the slight movement of a joystick, the line was released and flew about 30 feet each time. The exhilaration on his face with each successful cast was contagious. I smiled watching him deal with the fishing pole like a pro. Adjusting the tension on the device, he could change the distance of the cast, fine-tuning it as he went along.

I turned back to see the other man still dejectedly looking down at the ground, lost in thought. There was a striking contrast between these two people. There is an expression that rang true for me in that moment: "If we're not careful where we allow our thoughts to take us, we will always get more of what we don't want."

I pass many people in wheelchairs every day—on the sidewalks or in the halls of Craig Hospital—and most have a smile on their face. They've seemingly reached the point of accepting their current circumstance and have begun the process of moving on. I am not implying that they have given up hope of recovery, merely that they have accepted where they are at this moment. They have resolved to make the most of their rehabilitation. I suspect that some arrived there quickly, while for others, it took longer.

While exiting the park, I turned to look back at the dejected man. He had since departed. No doubt the sadness that clung to him like a shadow followed him as he left. Thoughts of him, though, stayed with me throughout the day.

Late that afternoon Ty, Angela, and I went outside. He has amazed the staff with his ability to maneuver the electric wheelchair, his "temporary" mode of transportation. We ended up in the center of a small park next to a small goldfish pond. The trickling sound of the water was soothing.

We sat there for a half an hour or so. I spent the time watching the goldfish. There were six of them; five were very active, constantly in search of morsels of food, while one was hunkered over in a corner. It was smaller in stature and had a different, nondescript gray color. Like a chameleon, it blended in with the dingy hues of the pond walls. It constantly inched backward into its recess, where the walls and floor of the corner space helped obscure it from view, offering a false sense of protection. Occasionally, one of the other goldfish would come over and nudge it, almost as if it were beckoning this solitary fish to join the others. But it would respond instead by withdrawing even deeper into its hiding place. Lao-tzu once said, "If you do not change direction, you may end up where you are heading."

The difference I noticed was that the other five fish were in constant forward motion. Never once did I see any of them swimming in a backward direction, nor did I see them ever remain stagnant. They were looking ahead, moving along in their lives. They were in constant search of food, seeking nourishment and that which would improve the outlook of their future. They reminded me of the guy casting his fishing pole earlier that day. In sharp contrast was the lonely fish, isolated and paralyzed with fear. Frozen in the dark corner of his solitary retreat, he and the dejected man who hunkered in the corner of the park shared a similar sad space.

For each, it was his own choice.

PATIENCE AND HOPE

(August 10th)

An important part of music lies in the space between two notes. The tendency is to rush to play the next note prematurely without first allowing the resonance of the preceding ones to fully develop. By including that gap, patience reveals the beauty of music that's otherwise missed. As L. B. Cowman once wrote in *Streams in the Desert,* "There is no music during a musical rest, but the rest is part of the making of the music. In the melody of our life, the music is separated here and there by rests. During those rests, we foolishly believe we have come to the end of the song."

Sadly, in today's world patience is a forgotten virtue. We live in a culture of instant oatmeal, fast foods, faster Internet access, and news outlets competing to provide almost instantaneous coverage of tragedies

24/7. Our fast-paced society focuses on instant gratification. We demand immediate results and consider it a failure if our projected timelines aren't met. Unfortunately, this is what we're teaching our children as well.

It should come as no surprise that when faced with adversity, we expect resolution to operate on a similar fast track. We need to be reminded that God did not create humans as instant beings. Certain things take time to unfold: we spend nine months gestating in our mother's womb; it takes us more than 13 years to reach puberty. Some changes require an entire lifetime, or longer.

The concept of patience is highly valued and woven into the fabric of most major faiths. According to Dr. Reuven Firestone, the Jewish Talmud teaches that, "Patience in God helps us to find the fortitude to deliver ourselves and our fellows from the evils that seem to be an inherent part of real life." An Islamic belief is that Allah is with those who remain patient, specifically during suffering.

When faced with a catastrophic injury such as Tyler's, being patient is of utmost importance. It's much like being thrust into a totally darkened room. The natural tendency is to frantically attempt escaping the darkness regardless of how blinded you are by it. The search for the exit will more than likely be futile. On the other hand, through the practice of patience, allowing one's eyes to adjust to the darkness enables him or her to see the terrain in a much different light.

The Divine doesn't demand patience as a punishment; rather, God uses it to bring us back to our humanity. The grace of God takes time. We must learn to slow down our expectations and resist the pressures of the instant society mentality. Patience teaches us discipline and provides the necessary amount time for understanding to occur. It can temper anger and renew endurance in the face of suffering. Patience can still the heart and quiet the mind while renewing the spirit.

PEOPLE OFTEN ASK ME HOW I COPE and where I find the strength to endure trying times such as these. The answer is simple—it lies in *hope.* Hope is what sustains us through the storm, this period of seemingly insurmountable adversity. It supports faith in the unknown, offering us the belief in that which has yet to be revealed. Hope is the promise that a positive outcome is within our grasp.

Yesterday, hope arrived at our son's door. Her name was Laurie Hillman. She shared her story with Ty. After she was injured in an accident, she was unable to move her arms or legs; she was tethered to a ventilator. She felt total hopelessness upon her discharge from Craig Hospital. As a single mother with a seven-year-old daughter, her options were quite limited, her circumstances overwhelming.

For over an hour, she related to us the story of her journey. At one point, the doctors told her unequivocally that she would be quadriplegic for life and that she should just get used to it. Her answer to them was patience and perseverance, fueled by hope. When Laurie bid us farewell, she promised to return again to see him. She stood up and *walked* out of the room, leaving in her wake an uplifted Tyler Gordon.

It is hope that enables us to embrace the required patience that is born out of the confidence that a goal is achievable. We must practice being infinitely hopeful and patient, never being dissatisfied with the speed or manner in which our healing arrives.

"God sends us times of forced leisure by allowing
sickness, disappointed plans, and frustrated efforts.
He brings a sudden pause in the choral hymn of our
lives, and we lament that our voices must be silent.
. . . Yet how does a musician read the rest?
He counts the break with unwavering precision
and plays his next note with confidence,
as if no pause were ever there."

— L. B. COWMAN

THE ROAD LESS TRAVELED

(August 13th)

Do you remember as a youngster going to the carnival that came to town once a year? There was an exhilarating ride with cars propelled by electricity delivered from a pole that reached up to the ceiling. Each car had a steering wheel, and with sparks flying off the ceiling, they glided on a smooth, greased surface. The object was to bump into the other cars, knocking them off their course, hence the name "bumper cars."

Life is like a bumper-car ride. One moment we're traveling down the road of life without a care in the world. The road is well paved and the ride is smooth. We are in control, enjoying but perhaps not fully appreciating the beauty of the passing scenery. Suddenly, a collision knocks us off course. The abruptness of the impact might send us reeling, careening out of control. We veer onto a different, unexpected, and often frightening new path. The direction of our life becomes vastly different than what it had been a mere moment before the crash. Whether this bump in the road is due to a failed relationship, the death of a loved one, a job lost, or, in Ty's case, a car accident, status quo is disrupted.

Our new course might be fraught with fear and uncertainty as we find ourselves lost in an uncharted landscape. How will we ever find our way back to our familiar and safe path? Is it even possible to return to it? And, if so, would it ever feel the same?

If only we had a good global positioning system to help us find our way. For those of us who are directionally challenged and happen to own a GPS, if we've ever taken a wrong turn, the voice prompts us by saying, "Recalculating." After a while, with a few suggested adjustments, we're usually directed back on track.

How each of us recalculates once we're knocked off course depends on the particular GPS we choose. Our travel agent and itinerary might differ depending on our religious background, upbringing, or experiences. Many paths are available to us. Some routes will lead to places of further isolation, while others will prove to be more promising.

OUR SON'S PATH HAS CERTAINLY been dramatically altered. His bumper car is now careening down a very foreign lane, one he never fathomed he would travel. As he attempts to regain control of the vehicle, his GPS is saying, "Tyler, recalculate . . . recalculate." The GPS knows that his injury is not the end of the road. It is just a detour in his path. This new road, although unfamiliar, is a course that will ultimately enrich him beyond imagination. It will strengthen and enlighten him for having traveled it.

The Road Not Taken

Two roads diverged in a yellow wood,
And sorry I could not travel both
And be one traveler, long I stood
And looked down one as far as I could
To where it bent in the undergrowth;

Then took the other, as just as fair,
And having perhaps the better claim,
Because it was grassy and wanted wear;
Though as for that the passing there
Had worn them really about the same,

And both that morning equally lay
In leaves no step had trodden black.
Oh, I kept the first for another day!
Yet knowing how way leads on to way,
I doubted if I should ever come back.

I shall be telling this with a sigh
Somewhere ages and ages hence:
Two roads diverged in a wood, and I—
I took the one less traveled by,
And that has made all the difference.

— ROBERT FROST

LESSONS
LEARNED

(August 14th)

Life has a way of offering to us that which we need the most. Often we may not appreciate the importance of a particular experience until a certain point, perhaps later in life.

Pardon my French, but shit happens! We all know that. Why these things happen has confounded some of the wisest people who have lived on this planet. Throughout recorded history, many have contemplated the question, *Why is this happening to me?* I first contemplated it as a young man when my father endured a painfully horrific death due to prostate cancer. He was a prince among men, and from my perspective as a 22-year-old, I couldn't come to grips as to why a good God would allow such a gentle man to suffer in such an inhumane fashion. It would take me decades of searching until I stumbled upon an understanding.

All too often, when confronted with adversity, we tend to blame someone or something else for our misfortune. God might become the recipient of that displeasure. If not the one being blamed, often we ascribe harsh conditions in our lives to God's will. Some believe that He is punishing us for evil deeds we've committed in the past; thus, we deserve the stuff that comes our way.

I am certain that individuals who have sustained serious injuries from an accident must ask themselves, *Why me?* In the circumstance of someone tragically injured as a result of a mistake made by another, perhaps a drunk driver or a stray bullet, that question likely takes on a totally different context.

Now that the dust has begun to settle a bit in our lives, what has been left behind are the troubling questions: Why Tyler? Why us? Why me?

FIVE MONTHS BEFORE TY'S ACCIDENT, Britt called me from Colorado asking for advice. Her college roommate, Jennifer Shoe, had been diagnosed with metastatic malignant melanoma. Despite aggressive treatment, the cancer had continued to spread throughout her body, and a large tumor had settled on her spine. Pressure from it had damaged her spinal cord, resulting in young Jennifer becoming paralyzed from the waist down.

Jennifer was an avid sports enthusiast, and she and Britt had that and much more in common. They had lived together as best friends for five years while attending college at East Carolina University. They shared a mutual love of snowboarding and helped their ECU snowboarding team win second place in the national women's snowboarding competition in 2007, an interesting feat seeing how there usually isn't snow in North Carolina like there is in Colorado!

Britt and Jennifer shared something else very special: a love and mutual respect for one another. Perhaps what bonded them so closely was that they also shared the same birthday: June 24, 1985.

Jennifer was well aware that her cancer treatment had become ineffective. Knowing this would likely be her last opportunity to spend time with her best friend, Jennifer had called Britt. Her wish was to travel to Durango for a weeklong visit. Britt called me wondering what I thought she should do.

I explained to her that as a paraplegic, Jennifer would have very special needs. The house Britt and Ty shared was not wheelchair accessible. There would be bathroom issues, and I shared with her my concerns as to whether the Durango hospital was equipped to handle major neurological complications should they arise during the visit. I was also protectively concerned about how Britt and Ty would respond if an emergency should occur. After weighing all the pros and cons, I suggested to Britt that she discourage Jennifer from coming.

Well, Britt chose not to heed my advice. I must admit retrospectively that I am glad she did not. Instead of what I had projected might happen, a beautiful week transpired, the memories of which are forever emblazoned in each of their memory banks. Britt and Ty were able to observe Jennifer's fiancé, Dave Mercer, as he provided the most basic of needs for the woman he loved. I am certain that my children initially thought they could never do what they saw Dave doing, but over the course of the week, they were fortunate to see firsthand that with the power of unconditional love, anything is possible. Jennifer and Dave had offered a beautiful lesson to Britt and Ty.

Three months after her visit, Jennifer peacefully crossed over to the other side of life. Even as she transitioned, she continued to inspire those who surrounded her in the circle of her life.

Ten months before Ty's accident, I was helping plan our 40th high school reunion. I had grown up in Louisville,

Kentucky, and was looking forward to reconnecting with former classmates, many of whom I hadn't seen in over four decades. While looking through my yearbook, I came upon a picture of my very first girlfriend, Marcia. We were quite the hot ticket way back in fourth grade. Our infatuation lasted all of about 2 years; our friendship, however, endured for 50.

I had not spoken to Marcia in years. When I found her number, I decided to give her a call. Someone else answered the phone, and after a few minutes, I heard a weak voice on the line say, "Hello?"

I asked, "Are you going to save the last dance for me at our reunion?"

Recognizing my voice, she replied, "Oh, Terry, I wish I could, but . . ." her voice trailed off. "I have a few health issues that keep getting in my way."

I had planned a trip to Louisville the following week to visit with family and asked if I might stop by to see her. She agreed.

When I arrived at their home, her husband, Curt Tofteland, greeted me at the front door. Entering the den, I found Marcia seated in a fully electric wheelchair. She could barely shrug her shoulders and had very minimal ability to rotate her head. Sadly, that was the extent of her ability to move. As I watched Curt attend to her, I envisioned what his life must have been like as the primary caregiver. I wondered if I would have the fortitude to do the same.

Marcia and I spent three glorious hours together. She shared with me some of her life's journey. She had been diagnosed with multiple sclerosis 25 years earlier. She had been a dancer and an actress, having worked in New York City in off-Broadway productions. The relentless disease she had contracted left her once well-tuned body severely disabled. In the course of our conversation, she described the mammoth challenges she'd faced, the suffering she experienced missing out on many of life's simple pleasures. But she also sprinkled into her description some of the obstacles she'd overcome and the special triumphs she'd achieved.

I asked Marcia if she was able to ascribe any meaning to the pain and suffering she'd endured. She pondered the question for a moment and responded, "Yes, enlightenment. This experience has propelled me to a much higher place."

Despite the pain of her physical condition, she shared with me that she wouldn't change one single thing about her life. "I am actually grateful for my disease, Terry," she said. "It has taught me more about myself than I ever could have found out otherwise. I learned how not to reject the pain of my adversity—how not to deny or ignore the hurt, but to embrace it as a precious gift from the Divine. I've found that by working through my turmoil, I've been able to discover goodness within the hardship and, more important, what lies beyond the suffering."

It was obvious to me that the lessons learned by Marcia had resulted in a significant transformation for her. Through her suffering, she had discovered an elevating understanding of life. She had reached a level that allowed her to change the question from *Why me?* to the profound *Why not me?*

I left my old friend that afternoon in awe of her strength and wisdom, thinking to myself, *Imagine being thankful for a disease that had ravaged your body!* The very disease that caused Marcia so much pain turned out to be the vehicle of her deliverance.

For some, crises define life. For others, like Jennifer and Marcia, they refine life.

Little did Britt, Tyler, and I appreciate the importance of the lessons our friends had offered to us in their final curtain calls. We had been given a precious gift that would provide us tools we could use when our own challenges arose, challenges that lay just around the bend.

HE AIN'T HEAVY, HE'S MY BROTHER

(August 16th)

This morning while walking through Washington Park, I spoke with my mother on the phone. She commented on how difficult it must be to cope with the burden of Ty's circumstance. She asked me, "Don't you just feel like curling up in a ball and hiding?"

I meditated for a long while on her question. Yes, there are times I wish I could curl up or just run away. Indeed, I would love to escape this nightmare. But the reality is that I'm the leader of the band. There's no one else to shoulder the load.

I RECALL YEARS AGO WHILE DATING ANGELA, when she, her brother Eric, and I embarked on a backpacking expedition in the Red River Gorge in Kentucky. Eric, an outdoor enthusiast, had just purchased a new backpack, one that balanced the weight of his equipment evenly between his shoulders and waist. I donned his old equipment, which was not nearly as user-friendly, and my wife carried a smaller backpack. Fifteen minutes into our three-day trek, Angela twisted her ankle on a tree root. With her ankle wrapped, she was able to continue—but only if I took on her burden. So I tied her backpack to mine as we continued deeper into the gorge.

The trail Eric had mapped out for us was literally up one steep hill and down another. After just a few hours, I was thoroughly exhausted to the point of near collapse! While I considered myself to be in pretty good physical condition, I had never engaged in a challenge quite as grueling as this. I had no idea how I'd survive another three days of this not-so-fun communion with nature.

In his backpack, Eric carried the tents and some utensils; my load, now including Angela's, included all the rest of the provisions we would need to survive the wilderness. I resolved that failure was simply not an option. I wish I could tell you that the impetus to continue the difficult hike was based on a noble mantra of never giving up; it was not. Ego had nothing to do with it— but I wasn't about to let Angela's brother, the young whippersnapper he was, outdo me! Plus, there was this issue of trying to impress my girlfriend. Okay, so a little bit of ego played into it.

In order to persevere, I remember playing a mind game with myself. In my imagined scenario, Eric and I were survivalists on a rescue mission to locate and save a woman who had been missing for over a week, lost deep in a jungle. We had successfully tracked her down and were now on our way back, within three days of returning her to safety. This imagined tale allowed me to stick it out and ultimately make it out of the Red River Gorge.

THERE IS A STORY ABOUT TWO BUDDHIST MONKS who were trekking through the Himalayas on a journey back to their monastery. It was during a bitterly cold winter, and a powerfully strong wind was gusting. They both knew that if they couldn't reach the safety of their monastery before nightfall, they would surely perish in the frozen tundra.

As they trudged step-by-step along the tortuous and icy path, they heard a cry for help off to their right. Peering over a steep cliff, they could barely see a man who had fallen from the path, injured so badly that he could not move.

The first monk looked at his companion and implored, "We must leave him where he lies. God has obviously delivered this man his fate based on his own karma. It is his challenge, not ours. We must continue on our way to the monastery if we are to survive."

The second monk, peering back down the jagged ravine at the injured man, shook his head no and replied to his friend, "You forge ahead. God has delivered me here to help a brother in need."

As his friend continued on the path, the second monk began the dangerous descent down to where he was able to lift the injured man onto his back and slowly climb back to the path at the top of the embankment. He then continued on the ever-darkening trail, uncertain now whether or not he would make it to the monastery with this added burden.

After many hours of walking in the darkness of night, off in the distance he finally saw the faintly glimmering lights of his cloister. As he approached, he stumbled over something on the path. Kneeling down, he found the first monk, who had collapsed and frozen to death just a few hundred feet from the monastery entrance. Mustering what little energy he had remaining, he struggled back to his feet and staggered the rest of the way home. He had succeeded in carrying a brother to safety.

Since Tyler's injury and the ensuing ordeal that has followed, I haven't once perceived this as a burden. This morning, as I continued on my walk through Washington Park, contemplating the concept of burden, a song from the '60s began playing in my mind. I found myself unable to get the tune out of my head, so I hummed it as I continued along the path. As I looked out onto the lake, I watched a swan float past me effortlessly, carrying a baby cygnet on her back.

The lyrics of the song gently rose to the surface. And as they did so, I marveled at the recall capacity of the brain. I hadn't thought about or heard this song in years, yet there it was! Maybe the old man isn't as senile as the kids often suggest. The words of the song "He Ain't Heavy, He's My Brother" rang true to me.

One of Webster's definitions of *brother* is "one related to another by common ties or interests." Although I am Tyler's father, we are brothers in arms, sharing a common purpose, a mutual goal: his healing.

And like the second monk, I believe God has delivered me to this spot in order to help a brother in need.

> *"I sought my soul, but my soul I could not see.*
> *I sought my God, but my God eluded me.*
> *I sought my brother, and I found all three."*

— **Author Unknown**

107

MAN OF STEEL

(August 20th)

As the story created by Jerry Siegel and Joe Shuster goes, an infant boy was rocketed to Earth by his scientist father mere moments before the destruction of their planet, Krypton. On a Kansas farm, a couple raised this child as Clark Kent.

Early in his life, he displayed superhuman capabilities. As a young man, he disguised himself as a mild-mannered reporter who dedicated himself to humanity by fighting for "truth, justice, and the American way." Faster than a speeding bullet, more powerful than a locomotive, and able to leap tall buildings in a single bound, he became our hero.

Otherwise invulnerable, Superman did, however, have an Achilles' heel. His weakness was kryptonite, a glowing green rock. When exposed to it, he experienced immediate pain, becoming debilitated from its effects, which significantly reduced his strength, in essence neutralizing his special powers.

When I was a youngster, the chink in Superman's armor first became apparent to me when George Reeves, the original Superman on the television series of the 1950s, committed suicide.

Then came Christopher Reeve, who catapulted into stardom in the early 1980s by portraying this superhero on the silver screen. He epitomized strength and fortitude. Just like the man of steel, Reeve was invincible and indestructible. Seemingly nothing could harm him. But in a tragic twist of fate, this super man was brought down, not from exposure to kryptonite, but by a fall from a horse during an equestrian event. Reeve sustained a significant spinal-cord injury that resulted in the same effect as that glowing green rock, the paralysis of his young and chiseled body.

Albert Einstein once said, "In the middle of every difficulty lies opportunity." Christopher Reeve's story didn't end with his injury—it began. Rising above adversity, he established the Christopher & Dana Reeve Foundation. Their mission is to find a cure for spinal-cord injuries and improve the quality of life of those living with paralysis. Leading by example, he demonstrated that even in the throes of paralysis, there remain choices. One can live in a state of self-doubt and fear, remaining forever frozen in place or forging ahead regardless of perceived limitations. This Superman mentality enabled Reeve to persevere and leap tall buildings despite his injury.

But there exists another less favorable facet of the Superman mentality. It's called ego. Ego tries to convince us that we are indestructible, creating a false sense of invincibility. In self-cherishing fashion, we egotistically worship our bodies. Our superficial appearance comes to define us. Some take this to an extreme, consuming muscle-enhancing supplements such as creatine and anabolic steroids to achieve Superman status with Incredible Hulk–like strength. Others have plastic surgery or get Botox injections in pursuit of Western society's obsessive image of youth and beauty.

This is not meant to imply that we shouldn't take care of the bodies we inhabit. From 1 Corinthians 6:19: "Do you not know that your bodies are temples of the Holy Spirit, who is in you . . . ?" Our bodies are temples, but the reverence should not be mistakenly attached to vanity. Our bodies are really not ours anyway; they are on loan to us from the Universe. Nature is the landlord, and our stewardship lasts but a blink of an eye. We must be cautious not to place too much importance on the rental property.

Inside of us there are really two selves. One resides in the material plane, where, if we allow, the ego commands a lot of attention. The other is our spiritual self. It resides in a place of much higher consciousness. To access this higher realm, it is necessary to control the ego, putting it in its proper place. We are so much more than our bodies. I imagine Christopher Reeve, as he coped with paralysis, came to view his fractured frame as only a thin veil of his true self. As he humbly relinquished ego, his invisible spiritual essence percolated to the surface where it germinated, blossomed, and ultimately flourished.

We should embrace this super man's example, for it was with humility that he was able to soar to an advanced place, reaching that higher level of consciousness where he overcame what others had erroneously considered to be the tragedy of his life.

LOSING BALANCE

(August 21st)

I witnessed a beautiful sunset this evening from Washington Park near Craig Hospital. As I looked westward, the sun was gently bidding farewell to the day as it slipped behind the glorious mountain range. I sat down on the grass and meditated with my eyes open, concentrating on my breath. Breath awareness is one of the best ways I've learned to experience the *now*. Conscious breathing calms and centers me, allowing me to commune with my inner self.

With each breath, the intensity of the sun's rays diminished. I felt my exhales gently pushing the sun away. The cool Colorado air caressed me as the sun, cresting in reverse of daybreak, disappeared as night began to fall.

The silhouetted ridges of the mountains glowed from behind. The beauty was breathtaking. I imagined what the other side of the mountain must look like, still bathed in the radiance of sunlight. But as my side of the mountain range was darkening, I watched in absolute awe.

I envisioned myself on the crest of the tallest peak. Attempting to balance on that unstable terrain, precariously trying to maintain my equilibrium, I felt like a drunkard trying to walk a straight line. I desperately wanted to stay in the sunlight, in that place of illumination. Unsteady and almost queasy with vertigo, I felt myself being drawn instead toward the opposite side. Trying not to believe what my eyes and senses were telling me, the pull was definitely toward the frightening cliffs of darkness.

As the dark side pulled at me, I placed my intention on the Light. I soon realized that the pull of gravity was the same on both sides of the mountain peak. Once I refocused, balancing became much easier and my breathing slowed.

Earlier today, I practiced Bikram yoga. The instructor guided us through a 90-minute series of 26 balancing postures, each performed twice. In a yoga frame of mind, I can let go of everything on either side of the now. Today, however, during many of the poses, I found it difficult to maintain my equilibrium. I struggled, losing the focus of being in the moment, and slipped into the space of worrying about the future, even though it was only a minute away. I found myself questioning my fortitude. Having failed the previous few poses, I began doubting whether I would be able to strike and maintain the next one, or the one after that.

Ultimately, I was able to break the cycle of worrying thoughts. I was able to return to the present moment, finding balance once again in the breath. I began concentrating on the cleansing breath of life, which rejuvenates not only me, but everything in the cosmos. The word *yoga* is derived from the Sanskrit root *yuj,* which means "to unite, to join in conjunction." The exhaled breath carries moisture from my lungs, which then coalesces with all of the moisture ever created, everywhere. It will become one with other droplets, condensing to become a rain cloud that one day will empty itself, nurturing everything that has the potential for growth. Therein lies the balance of nature.

As my evening meditation came to a peaceful end, my breath pushed the sun one last time as it crested over the sleepy mountain. Another glorious day was ending, the balance of nature's continuity intact. It is with the same deep cleansing breath that I offer myself to you, to my son, and to all that is.

RUNNING BLIND

(August 25th)

Belief systems can change in an instant. Newly discovered truths replace previously believed facts. Around 1513, Copernicus's calculations proved that the sun, and not the Earth, was the center of our solar system. This new discovery challenged the very foundation of the Roman Catholic Church, which did not respond very kindly to his "disruptive" revelation. Eventually, however, it became accepted fact.

On July 26, 1852, Charles Westhall established the benchmark for the mile run, 4 minutes and 28 seconds. Thereafter, for more than 100 years, the "fact" was that no one believed that a human being could run a mile in less than four minutes. But on May 6, 1954, Roger Bannister broke the four-minute mile, running it in 3 minutes and 59.4 seconds. How? It was simple. He approached his goal logically. He convinced his mind that the four-minute mile was an attainable goal.

Within eight weeks, that record was broken, and then broken again. The fact had changed. What was considered impossible actually happened, and the doors opened for others to run a mile even faster. Many athletes have since accomplished this great feat, in part because the belief has shifted.

The other day in the park, I marveled at several disabled people. One was a young boy with cerebral palsy. He was riding on an adapted cycle fitted just for him. He was with a group of other disabled individuals who were peddling their cycles with their arms. The joy on his young face made it clear that he was savoring every moment of this accomplishment.

I love to watch people. I especially enjoy the messages on their T-shirts, which usually give me some insight into their personalities. Behind me someone called out, "Excuse us," and a lady ran past me. I saw a rope tied around her waist. Tethered to her, a man ran in perfect synchrony approximately eight feet behind her. As they passed me, I noticed the back of his shirt, which read BLIND RUNNER.

He was blind all right, but he knew right where he was going! It must be exhilarating to know where you're headed. He wasn't looking back; he didn't care where he had been. He forged ahead, one stride at a time. I tried to imagine the difficulty of running without *seeing* where I was going. This blind man totally relied on his friend to show him the way, to run his interference for him.

Just then, two individuals on Rollerblades whisked past me, one right in front of the other. The guy who followed dangerously close behind the leader was drafting off his friend's energy, his alignment reducing the overall effect of the drag. In an instant, they changed positions; the leader became the follower. Each gained strength from the other.

Several of Tyler's physicians have conveyed what they believe to be fact: that he will never walk again. But as Roger Bannister proved so many years ago, the mind is the limit. Anything is possible if the belief that it can be done precedes it! All we need is a reason to change that belief.

None of us is smart enough to be pessimistic about our son's potential for recovery. After all, who can account for all the factors involved in the process of healing? Certainly those of us in the practice of medicine cannot. Complete recovery is not out of the realm of possibility. As Michelangelo once cautioned, "The greatest danger for most of us is not that our aim is too high and we miss it, but that it is too low and we reach it."

As Ty's marathon unfolds, he will likely have to face many uncertainties along his path. Because he's running blind, he probably won't be able to see what lies in his way. But we will forge ahead of him, leading him while scouting potential obstacles. We will help him navigate around the potential impediments. Tyler will gain strength and one day, with a proud smirk on his face, whisk past us; and with newly found vigor, he'll begin drafting for us.

WHERE IS THE LOVE?

(August 27th)

Cards, e-mails, and calls from family members, friends, acquaintances, and even total strangers have heartened Tyler. The energy of the many well-wishers has been as strong as the forces of nature—gravity, wind, and sunshine all expressed as love. Love and energy are inextricably connected. It is through them that we as humans unite, even if we do not personally know one another.

I have never seen gravity, but watching an acorn fall from a tree, I have noticed its effects. I cannot see the wind, but I watch as the flowers gently sway in its wake. In similar fashion, although we cannot directly see the love we're receiving, the Gordons have felt its soothing energy.

Have you ever wondered where love resides? For centuries, the heart has been considered its source. Why else would this feeling of love or, for that matter, heartache, seem to emanate from the area in our chest where the heart lies?

Historically, intellect was considered separate from emotions, even located at a different place in the body. The heart and brain have traditionally been pitted against one another as the controller of the human psyche. Plato considered the brain to be the center of human essence, believing that emotions were like "wild horses that had to be reined in by the intellect." Aristotle, on the other hand, viewed the heart as the seat of the soul.

Interestingly, scientists have recently discovered that the heart is more than just a pump. Research has confirmed that this organ has a complex nervous system independent of the brain. It possesses its own circuitry, consisting of more than 40,000 nerve fibers that are capable of detecting things such as circulating hormones and neurochemicals, substances that govern electrical impulses. This functional "heart brain" (coined by neurocardiologist, Dr. J. Andrew Armour) influences not only the heart, but impacts some brain function as well. In addition, this heart brain oversees many of the bodily functions previously ascribed to the brain. In other words, the heart has a mind of its own. But we all knew that!

Forgetting the controversy of where it resides, the capacity to love remains an integral part of the human experience. Regardless of from where love originates, opening the heart to it reveals the most precious treasures of life.

We are deeply grateful to everyone for their thoughts, their prayers, their phenomenal energy, and especially their gift of love.

"Someday, after we have mastered the wind, the waves, the tide and gravity, we shall harness for God the energies of love; and then for the second time in the history of the world man will have discovered fire."

— PIERRE TEILHARD DE CHARDIN

EASE ON DOWN THE ROAD

(August 31st)

During World War II, a U.S. ambassador was assigned to a European embassy. One day he received a wire from the States informing him that his only child had just died in an automobile accident. An embassy party had been planned for that evening, and he was to be the host. The ambassador decided to attend the event despite the tragic news he had just received.

As his guests arrived that evening, word quickly spread about his loss. Many couldn't believe that he would be so insensitive as to attend a festive party the very night of his son's untimely death. At one point, he overheard one of the guests expressing her displeasure with his decision to attend. During the welcoming speech for his guests, he shared, "I loved my son with all my heart and will miss him terribly. But this I know: Sooner or later I will need to get over it. I have simply decided that it will be sooner."

THE OTHER DAY I TRAVELED HOME TO OHIO. While checking in at the airport, an engaging man caught my attention. His brilliant smile radiated from an enviable inner peace and happiness. I wondered how he achieved that state of mind . . . in a wheelchair, no less.

I eavesdropped on the conversation he was having with the female ticket agent, and found myself smiling at the interaction. From his seated position, he was making fun of how tall she was. She really wasn't tall at all, but appeared to be from his vantage point. He told her he had always been attracted to women who towered over him.

When I finished checking in, I looked around and found him next to the gate. As I approached, he looked up and smiled. I introduced myself, and he said that his name was Jeffrey Blasband. Over the past several days, my emotions had been hovering just below the surface. With tears welling up in my eyes, I told him, "I wish my son could see your smile." Then from nowhere, I broke down crying. I was embarrassed to cry in front of a total stranger, but somehow I knew it was okay.

Once I composed myself, he asked me about Tyler. I described the nature of his injury, and I conveyed his immense suffering at having been so physically active and now paralyzed.

Jeffrey looked down, slowly nodding his head. He knew exactly what Ty was going through. He had been at a similar place 20 years before. As a teenager, he'd been shot in the back. He knew immediately that he was paralyzed from the waist down. He too had been physically active, and that made his recovery all the more challenging. He explained, "I'm not going to tell you that the first two or three years were easy for me— they weren't. They were pure hell." And then Jeffrey simply, but profoundly, said, "But you know what? At some point Tyler is just going to have to get over it."

The words resonated with me. At some point Ty *will* just have to get over it. He may decide to do so in three days or in a month. It might be another five years until he reaches the point of acceptance. It may take him a lifetime. But whenever it happens, a shift *will* occur. When he decides to change the way he looks at his circumstance, his circumstance will change. Only when that shift in consciousness occurs will he be able to move on with his life.

As I reflect on Jeffrey—and I have often since our "chance" meeting in the airport—the one thing that first drew my attention to him is a detail I no longer carry in my memory. When I envision him, recalling his appearance, I don't remember him as being seated in a wheelchair. The energy radiating from him conveyed that he was not wheelchair bound . . . he was wheelchair free.

The happiest people I know don't necessarily have the best of everything, but they make the best of everything they have. Or as Wayne Dyer once said: "There is no way to happiness—happiness is the way."

NOTHIN' EVER
LASTS FOREVER

(September 4th)

There was a full moon last night. When I awoke at 3:18 A.M., I stepped out onto the balcony in the silence of the cool summer night. It was a very peaceful moment. I was mesmerized by the clear reflection of the moon off the smooth surface of our lake. It made me pause as I reflected on my family's journey, where we've come from and where we're going.

It has been more than two months since Ty's accident. The moon has risen in the evening sky and disappeared over the horizon 69 times.

From our vantage point, we observe the ever-changing face of the moon as it orbits the earth. The moon never looks the same for any two consecutive nights. It reflects the bright rays from the sun in this cyclical change that has played out every single evening for millions of years. We have come to accept that change as a natural transition, demonstrating the impermanence of nature. After all, there is only one constant in life, and that is change. Everything is impermanent.

While back in Ohio this past week, I spent time working with David Petras—or, as we affectionately call him, "Davo." He's feverishly tearing down walls and rebuilding several rooms to facilitate Ty's needs once he returns home.

Last evening at home by myself, I went up to Ty's new bedroom and sat down on the floor. The changes being made to both his and the adjacent girls' rooms began to sink in. I felt sad reflecting on all the fond memories of those parts of the house, lamenting the demise of these individual spaces. The walk-in closet that was in Mattie-Rose and Laila's bedroom has now become part of Tyler's expanded room. Where the girls slept is his new bathroom. The appearance of these rooms has changed; they will never be the same.

Death can manifest in many ways. Like his room, Ty's physical form is quite different today than it was 69 moons ago. One can only imagine the dramatic impact such a drastic change will have on this 21-year-old's self-esteem and psyche. The perceived death of his physique has been as devastating to him as the death of a loved one might be to someone else.

I can only pray that one day he will free himself from the notion that his form defines who he is. I hope he will soon come to know that he is much more than his body. To the ego, this body and this life are extremely important, providing a false sense of continuity, of permanence. But in truth, nothing remains the same . . . ever. Our bodies are in a constant state of flux. Even our cells are constantly dying and being replaced by new, healthy cells every day. As such, we are not the same person from day to day; we aren't even the same from breath to breath.

Become totally empty.
Let your heart be at peace
Amidst the rush of worldly comings and goings,
Observe how endings become beginnings.

In this opening paragraph of the 16th verse of the Tao Te Ching, Lao-tzu urges us not to be afraid of impermanence. He encourages us to be ever mindful of the constancy of change. The cyclical harmony of impermanence always has been and always will be nature's way of continuing itself. Nothing is ever destroyed.

There is no such thing as the finality of death. Everything is simply . . . transforming.

"There would be no chance at all of getting to know death if it happened only once. But fortunately, life is nothing but a continuing dance of birth and death, a dance of change. Every time I hear the rush of a mountain stream, or the waves crashing on the shore, or my own heartbeat, I hear the sound of impermanence. These changes, these small deaths, are our living links with death. They are death's pulse, death's heartbeat, prompting us to let go of all things we cling to."

— SOGYAL RINPOCHE, *THE TIBETAN BOOK OF LIVING AND DYING*

Following each moon comes the dawn of a new day, unique and different from any other ever manifested. The impermanence of yesterday has paved the way for the endless possibilities of today. We should not grieve or lament change; we should embrace it as the blessing it is.

Thank you for the valuable lesson. Good night, moon.

HEALING HANDS

(September 6th)

Over the past few days, Tyler has been stuck in a bad funk. On several occasions he has pleaded with me, "Pops, I'm done here. Please let me go home . . . I just wanna go home." Stuck in a place somewhere between here and home, he didn't sleep well last night, voicing once again his desire to just go home. Reluctantly, he went to physical therapy, and during his one-hour lunch break came back to his room. After a few moments, we heard a gentle knock on the door.

While I was back home last week, an acquaintance had brought a friend named Bob to meet Tyler. This man had described to Angela that a number of years ago he had come to appreciate that he had been blessed with a powerful gift, one of hands-on healing.

During their initial encounter, Bob had shared with Angela that several days ago, he had experienced intense burning in his hands, a sign to him that there was work to be done with someone. At the time, he didn't know who that person would be.

It was during that first visit that Bob placed his healing hands on our son, and Tyler had definitely felt some changes in his own hands as a result.

Bob returned on this day of "funk," for some odd reason. He had simply been in the neighborhood, and felt compelled to come back to see Tyler again.

Upon hearing the knock on the door, we called out, "Come in." Our guest hesitantly entered the room, apologizing for his uninvited visit. He asked that if it was okay, he would like to share his healing hands once again.

Bob sat down behind Ty and gently placed his special hands on our son's shoulders, and they remained there for almost an hour. As I watched Bob, every so often he would cock his head, as if perceiving something. He'd then make the slightest adjustment in the positioning of his hands.

Angela and I could see the tension melting away from Tyler; he almost fell asleep with Bob's hands placed on him. When Bob finished, he stood up, thanked us for allowing him to "intrude," picked up his cup of coffee, and, as humbly as he had arrived, departed.

Why had he felt compelled to return today of all days? What had he hoped to accomplish? Neither are questions for which I have a clear answer. What I do know is that he shared a piece of himself with us while channeling Divine energy into our son, the fortunate beneficiary.

Shortly after Bob's departure, I was looking out the window when I saw him emerge from the front door of the hospital. As he exited, he paused for a moment, taking a sip of his coffee. He looked around at the trees and shrubs and lifted his head toward the crystal-blue sky. He took in a deep breath of the cool autumn air, and, with a bounce in his step, walked away.

I stretched my neck as I tried to keep him in sight for as long as possible, but too soon, he vanished from my view, and we never saw him again.

There have been so many beautiful people who have come in and out of our lives while here in Colorado—some, like Bob, only evanescently. I can only hope that we have in some way impacted their lives as richly as they have touched ours.

If we did not, our commitment is to pay it forward.

RENEGADE

(September 8th)

Yesterday the brilliance of Tyler's smile returned. Brief as it was, it appeared nonetheless. As the day progressed, his dry sense of humor trickled back to the surface from where it had been hibernating for far too long.

Having become quite adept at maneuvering his fully electric-powered wheelchair that was fitted just for him, Ty is now tooling around the hospital with ease. I'm awaiting his first wheelie! He did, however, inform me in no uncertain terms not to bother buying one of these "damn contraptions," as he fully intends *not* to require its services.

The physical and occupational therapists are both very pleased with Ty's progress these past two weeks. As he becomes more active, strength is returning to his body as it begins the task of recuperating.

I also sense a reemergence of his strong spirit, along with the fortitude that has defined him up to this point. No doubt, it will likely wax and wane over the course of his recovery. It might even go back into hiding at some point. But eventually, emerge it will.

Yesterday, Tyler took off in his wheelchair by himself—something, by the way, he is *not* supposed to do! But since when has that made a difference? I was crossing the street on my way back to our apartment, when I happened to look up. There he was on the third-floor bridge that connects the two wings of Craig Hospital. He was sitting there just looking up at the early-evening sky. *A penny for your thoughts?* I wondered as I stood in the middle of the street looking up at him. *I can't imagine what you're going through, Boosle Boy.*

One of the things I've always admired so much about my son has been his strength. I am not referring to his chiseled body. Call it bullheadedness, resolve, or independence, Ty has always demonstrated fortitude, an inner knowing, a depth of thought that I have admired for many years.

As parents, we attempt to guide our children as best we can, relying on our own experiences as the map. We hope to impart how to best navigate through this thing called life based on what *we* found to have worked for us. Often we strive, subconsciously perhaps, to make our children just like ourselves. But as Kahlil Gibran helped me articulate earlier in the book, children "come through you but not from you."

Tyler has always been his own man. He continues to display this resolve, which is a trait that I know will empower him as he deals with this injury. His path won't necessarily be the same one that I'd take; he'll forge ahead on one that is singularly his own.

Many individuals are convinced that they know the only way. Consider yourself as being at your ultimate destination. Now look around for all of your loved ones. Beckon them to you, encourage them to join you in this place of ultimate destiny. At this particular moment in time, each of those people who are dearest to you is in a different location. They can come to meet you at this special place, but the paths they must take will all be quite different.

The journey for each of us is a unique experience.

As I looked up one last time from the street at the renegade patient above, I smiled with pride as I saw Tyler Gordon's independence returning, *his* individual path unfolding.

Happy trails to you, Ty-Ty.

STRONG ENOUGH TO BEND

(September 10th)

Trees have played a prominent role in most religions and societies. In the Garden of Eden, the Tree of Knowledge had ten branches, each touched by a particular power of God. The Torah describes the Tree of Life as an example for living a powerful and joyous life. Egyptian mythology tells of gods obtaining their immortality from the sycamore tree. On the ark, Noah received the promise of the future for humankind from a dove carrying a branch of an olive tree in its beak.

Alice Walker taught me that "In nature, nothing is perfect and everything is perfect. Trees can be contorted, bent in weird ways, and they're still beautiful."

I've always had affection for trees. The magnetism of their energy has long attracted me. In their midst I feel a strong connection with Source.

Today, I was walking through Washington Park when I came upon an old shagbark hickory. From afar, this mammoth tree seemed to have been damaged, as it appeared twisted and contorted. A few branches stretched precariously out over the lake's edge.

As I approached, I could see the tree was intact; there was no damage. The loose-plated bark of this particular hickory is distinctive, making it appear to be falling apart or splintering to pieces. It reminded me of a giant fried blooming onion.

Even though they appear fragile, shagbark hickories are some of the toughest trees that exist. Their resilient wood is suitable for high-impact tools, and it's also a good source of firewood. Well grounded, their taproots penetrate deeply into the earth, making them extremely stable, even against the strongest of winds.

As I walked closer to this beautiful tree, I reached out and gently touched its bark, not wishing to disrupt any further its outer shell. I sat down for a while underneath its expansive limbs and then reclined against the base. Grounded by Mother Earth, I looked up through the hickory's green leaves at the clear blue sky. I listened to the far-off sounds of the park. I could feel the vibrant energy that was being emitted by this majestic tree. Connecting with such a powerful life force, one appreciates a sense of endurance. If you wrap your arms around the trunk of a tree, it wraps itself around you. The connectivity is astounding.

The similarities between this shagbark hickory and Tyler flooded my consciousness. The energy of the old tree is being shared with the cosmos, much like my son is sharing his energy with the Universe. His exterior may appear fragile like the shagbark's, but inside he remains as strong and resilient as the hard wood of the old hickory. Rooted in a strong foundation of love, Ty remains steadfast. Yes, winds may blow forcefully over, under, and through his branches, but his core strength will sustain him. He remains tall, stretching toward the sun.

Nature can be our teacher. If we seek her treasures, she clears our vision, illuminates our minds, and purifies our hearts. The whispering of the trees in the woods and the voices of nature reveal to us that God is in our midst. He has granted us the ability to hear the music of the world. In order to heed the messages, we must stop to savor these sounds.

THE RAINBOW CONNECTION

(September 18th)

We do not live separately. We are all interconnected and interdependent. Nothing exists in and of itself. As John Donne so eloquently described, "No man is an island, entire of itself; every man is a piece of the continent, a part of the main."

The other day, the therapeutic recreation department at Craig Hospital planned a fishing excursion to Island Lake near Denver. After the gear was loaded and all the participants' wheelchairs were secured, the specially equipped van departed on the adventure.

As we rode along, we got acquainted with one another. Each of the 15 patients had vastly different stories. Several described their unique journeys that lead them to Craig Hospital; others only listened as we became connected.

Synchronicity is always present. All we have to do is open our minds and eyes to its existence. Once we allow ourselves to be receptive, the natural flow of life unfolds before our eyes. We discover that life is not a random set of experiences; indeed, there are no coincidences. Matters of happenstance do not just occur. It was no mistake that we ended up at this point in time in the van together.

We arrived at our destination, an island in the middle of a large lake. My first thought was, *How are they going to get these people in wheelchairs from dry land to the island?* Then three fun-loving people showed me! One by one, the participants were loaded onto a pontoon boat that ferried us over to Windsor Island.

Several stellar employees from Craig Hospital accompanied us on this outing. Specially modified fishing equipment was available for those who could not use their arms and hands. One of the most energetic volunteers was a man whose hobby is adapting fishing gear. He worked with all of the participants, adjusting the equipment to their particular needs. The exuberance overflowed from him as he delighted in helping transform the disabled to enabled.

How this trip to Windsor Island all came about was inspiring. John Jensen, a former patient at Craig Hospital, had sustained a paralyzing spinal-cord injury as a young man. Told he would never walk again, he set about to prove the physicians and therapists wrong. Working with the staff, he succeeded and is now able to walk. In appreciation for those at Craig Hospital, John donates these excursions three times a year to currently hospitalized patients.

As he quietly observed the fruit of his contribution, a warm smile crossed John's face, conveying the gratitude he felt for life. His had been a long journey, one that had many peaks and valleys. He shared with me how surreal this experience was for him: "As I look around at these people in their wheelchairs, it's as if I'm observing myself at different stages of my own recovery. I envision what the future can hold for each of them, if only they'll believe in their recovery. The potential exists for each and every one of them." Although John well understood their disabilities, he appreciated the endless possibilities within their grasp if they choose to reach for them.

I WANDERED OFF BY MYSELF TO MEDITATE. Along a winding path I found a quiet place along the lake's edge. The surface of the lake was very still. I became just as tranquil, my thoughts dissipating to make way for the peaceful space of the stilled mind.

I threw a pebble into the water. It hit the still surface of the lake with a soft plop. Circular ripples spread out in all directions. As I watched them expand in an outward direction, I contemplated Tyler's car crash and the rippling effect it has had on so many lives.

People from all walks of life have expended their energy, as a cascade of activity generated by the accident resulted in responses from the highway-patrol officer who first arrived at the scene, the staff at the ER in Durango, the helicopter pilot and life-flight crew who safely transported Tyler to Denver, and the marvelous staff at both Swedish and Craig Hospitals. Assistance has come from housekeepers, technicians, nurses, and physicians charged with his care. All of these lives and many more have been touched and forever changed by the ripples emanating from my son's injury.

Everything we do—from our actions, to our words, and even our thoughts—generate similar ripples, which spread outward into the Universe. Because the impact of our ripples has everlasting consequences, we must be ever mindful of the energy we release.

As I slowly emerged from my meditative state, I opened my eyes to see that the surface of the lake was once again still. Off in the distance I could hear laughter and muted conversation as my new friends were gathering for dinner. I walked back to the pavilion, where everyone was already seated at tables preparing to dine. I joined them.

Some fed themselves, while a loved one or caregiver fed others. Looking around at the group, I appreciated that even though our appearances varied, despite the fact that we possessed different capabilities and had come from vastly different backgrounds, we were all connected at this moment just like the different colors of an exquisite rainbow. We were one. We were all enjoying the same great meal and sharing the marvelous energy of conversation that lasted for well over an hour.

Gradually, as the dialogue died down, it was replaced by the distant sound of crickets. We drew silent, mesmerized by a pristine sunset. Everyone marveled at the beauty of this moment as dusk approached, the day beginning its end. We were blessed to share this special time with each other.

At this point in time, there were no worries, no sadness or pain, only pure bliss. Being in harmony with the life force taps us into the energy that flows through every living thing. That evening on Island Lake, the rainbow connection allowed for that flow to course through us all.

It's difficult to appreciate the present moment when energy is wasted worrying about things that have happened in the past, or for that matter what might occur in the future. In the magic of this special moment, none of us was looking backward or forward. We were simply looking around. We were all connected in that present and exquisitely beautiful moment, enjoying the end of the day to the fullest. The Universe had brought us together, its purpose likely different for each of us. But the brief time we spent with one another, and the commonality we shared, was very special indeed.

On the trip home in the van, enveloped in the darkness of night, we each settled back into our own worlds. Not much was said . . . and it didn't have to be.

A CHANGE IS COMING

(October 7th)

The autumn morning sky of Denver was a cloudless azure, a stark contrast to the darkly etched mountains in the distance. Each day in Colorado, I marvel at the beauty of the magnificent Rockies. They may appear unchanged from day to day, but for the past week or so I have noticed a subtle difference. During the cool autumn nights, the Artist has gently stroked His canvas with a soft brush dipped in pure white snow. At first, it was just the whitened tips of the mountain peaks, but now snow is flowing down the mountainside, almost as if it were thick icing on a sticky bun.

Everywhere change is occurring. The days are getting shorter, the nights colder. The aspen leaves have begun turning yellow. The repeating refrains of nature, the seasonal changes we see, assure us of the continuation of life on Earth. Squirrels and chipmunks scamper around hoarding nuts. Every creature is preparing for the winter that will precede the spring. I even noticed a new sign near the lake at Washington Park: THIN ICE, KEEP OFF LAKE.

It is T-minus 16 days until our big change happens— our return to Ohio. We are scurrying around just like all the animals in the park. The staff at Craig continues to help us as we begin our home-going process, which seems strangely similar to that of the squirrels: We too are gathering and saving many precious nuggets of information. We are picking up on helpful hints and tools we will need to sustain us through a winter the likes of which we have never known. Yes, as a family, we have endured many winters before, but this one will most assuredly be different. It will require us to utilize new and much different resources.

"God is able to make all grace abound toward you; that ye, always having all sufficiency in all things, may abound to every good work."

— 2 CORINTHIANS 9:8

God has always provided for us whatever is needed. As such, there is no fear; paucity is of no concern.

The wide variety of "nuts" we are gathering will sustain the six of us during the cold, wintry days ahead. The only difference between the squirrels and us is that I don't believe we'll be doing much hibernating!

I'm sorry this entry is so short, but I've just seen another nut under a tree across the lawn. I'd better go grab it before it gets snatched up!

SWIMMING UPSTREAM

(October 12th)

It is T-minus 11 days and counting. Today is Angela's birthday. As you might imagine, she's not very enthusiastic about celebrating. In her beautifully selfless manner, she has redirected her birthday wishes for the benefit of another.

Arrangements are proceeding as planned here at Craig Hospital. We have absorbed much information, and much more is yet to come. Equipment has been ordered and is being shipped to our home in Ohio. Tomorrow, I leave for one last trip home to check on the preparations for our return. Soon our entire family will reunite where we belong, at home.

As this Colorado experience is winding down, I have reflected on each of the 104 days spent here.

Many emotions flood my mind. The other day, just before a cold spell hit Denver, I was walking once again around Washington Park—a place I will surely miss. Being able to walk its paths without being noticed has been a beautiful respite for me. When you go to a place where no one knows you, it's much easier to find yourself.

A creek courses through the park, connecting the two large lakes. I stopped on one of the bridges that crosses the water and watched a pair of ducks paddling around in search for food. What seemed to be the easiest route for them to take, following the current downstream, was not their chosen path. Instead, they were swimming upstream, struggling against a rather brisk current. I wondered why they chose to fight that current. Why not take a path of less resistance? I was amazed and perplexed.

In his book *Why Faith Matters,* Rabbi David J. Wolpe poses the question: "Do you believe that there is a mystery at the heart of the universe that we will never be able to fully understand, not through lack of effort but because it cannot be understood?" Over the past 104 days, many questions have scrolled through my mind. Several of them remain unanswered, and likely will remain so. After much contemplation and introspection, the most profound thing I have come to accept is that *why* the Gordons are facing this huge challenge is immaterial. What's more important is *how* we're overcoming it.

Like the two ducks, we too have spent the past three and a half months swimming upstream, often becoming exhausted by our efforts. There were times when fatigue overwhelmed us and we had to let go. The rush of the current carried us back downstream, where tumbling in the turbulence we lost precious ground that we'd previously gained. Once we reestablished our composure, we paddled right back to where we'd left off. We discovered that by moving upstream against the current, we've become invigorated by the effort and strengthened in a way we couldn't have otherwise achieved.

The quest for understanding continues even as we embark on this next leg of our journey home. We will use the blessings of this experience to gain the fullest appreciation possible of its purpose and meaning. As Rabbi Wolpe suggests, we may never come to fully *know* what that is. But one thing is for certain: as we continue our upstream adventure, we will grow along the way.

TWO WOLVES

(October 19th)

A Native American legend offers an invaluable lesson about life. While sitting by a campfire one evening, an old Cherokee brave was looking deeply into the fire's burning embers. His grandson walked up and sat down next to him, having come to ask for advice.

The young boy shared feelings of anger he had, directed at a friend who had done him an injustice. The old brave imparted the following wisdom:

"Grandson, let me tell you a story. I have also felt great anger and even hatred toward those who have taken so much from our land and given back so little. But hatred only wears *you* down. It does not affect your enemy.

"There is a battle that rages within me, within all people. The battle is between two wolves that live inside us. One is evil. This wolf is angry. He is filled with envy, jealousy, and resentment. Arrogant and greedy, he is full of hatred. He fights with everyone, sometimes for no reason at all. He cannot think clearly, because his hatred has overpowered him.

"The other wolf is good. He is full of joy, peace, love, and hope. He is benevolent in his generosity, humble in his compassionate approach. He lives in harmony with those around him and will only fight if it becomes absolutely necessary.

"Grandson, the battle between these two wolves often rages for many moons."

As they sat there in silence, watching the hot embers glow in the fire, the grandson contemplated his grandfather's words. After a while he asked, "Grandfather, which wolf wins?"

The old Cherokee smiled and simply replied, "Why, Grandson, the one you feed."

It is T-minus four days; the countdown continues toward October 23rd, our day of departure. For the past week or so, the two wolves have been waging a battle within me. The ferocity of their engagement intensifies daily. As the all-important date approaches, my thoughts have become more frenzied as I find myself falling into the trap of becoming more and more anxious about what lies ahead. Will I be able to rise to the challenge?

I remind myself that worrying doesn't help, but I still catch myself throwing morsels at each of the two wolves battling inside my mind. I watch them devour my food of thought, each using my energy quite differently. The evil wolf grabs at the bait, thrashing me from side to side. As his teeth dig in, he sucks from me every bit of energy, leaving me filled with turmoil, suffering, and anguish.

In stark contrast, his opponent offers generosity, love, and peace, infusing me with positive energy. He empowers me to achieve more than I ever could alone.

Each of us has free will. We decide whether to align with the empowering, uplifting, and positive high-energy patterns, or to become affected by those of negativity and low energy. From extensive kinesiology research, David R. Hawkins, M.D., Ph.D., describes in his book *Power vs. Force* the physical effects of positive and negative energy patterns. When we are empowered with positive energy, we are energized with positive "attractor patterns" and we flourish. Positive energy supports life and promotes health and happiness. The use of force, a negative energy pattern, promotes the opposite: weakness. This manifests as illness and perpetual turmoil. We must be very cautious of which wolf we choose to feed and nurture.

The reunion of our family back home in Ohio is right around the corner. I pray that our lives will soon return to some semblance of normalcy. I suspect life now will become a *new* normal, but there is comfort in knowing that we will join together to ward off the Big Bad Wolf.

In preparation for our travel day, may all the positive, empowering energy in the Universe assist Tyler on a safe and peaceful journey back to his lair.

PART III

THE SUNSHINE'S DANCING ON THE CLOUDS

A NEW BEGINNING

(October 23rd)

I left our rented apartment for the last time this morning. It was the dawn of a new day, the last day of our Denver experience. As the early sun was just beginning to appear over the horizon, a wave of melancholy flowed through me. I would sorely miss the Colorado sun. It had been my friend and my teacher. Along with nature, it had helped sustain me through periods of darkness. It had illuminated the way, offering me hope when I felt there was none. It's only fitting that my friend should be there blessing this new day with its radiance.

It is T-minus six hours and counting. *Today is the first day of the rest of our lives.* I never particularly liked this trite saying, even when it appeared ad nauseam affixed to everything back in the '60s. However, it does have some relevance as we prepare to leave the comfort zone of Craig Hospital and begin our lives anew back home in Richfield.

Departing is a bittersweet feeling, strangely similar to the conflicting emotions I experienced when I left home for college. While I was excited to be on my way with the anticipation of new independence, deep inside I realized life would never be the same again. A defining moment occurred when the door to our family home closed shut behind me. The lock mechanism engaged with a loud click, announcing that this door of my life had closed, never to open again. I found myself more frightened than I had anticipated. It took just one step for me to cross the threshold out of my previously comfortable life, just one step. In closing that door, it felt like I had burned my bridge before making it to the other side. As I embarked on this new path—the first day of the rest of my life—I was left with only one direction to walk, and that was . . . away.

There are similar feelings of apprehension, trepidation, regret, and even sadness as we prepare to leave the hospital this morning. These past four months, we have been nestled in the comforting care of many kind, generous, and professional individuals who dedicated themselves to the well-being of Tyler Gordon and his family. Their commitment to his rehabilitation has paved the way for us to continue on this path of recovery for Ty, and their thoughtfulness and expertise will be greatly missed. Although, as the staff has encouraged, "We'll only be a phone call away," it is simply terrifying knowing that when the door to Craig Hospital closes—clicking behind us just like the door of my family home all those years ago—we will be on our own.

The morning brought a flurry of activity, as last-minute instructions and preparations were made. Bags were packed and the final boxes were stuffed with accrued mementos and needed supplies.

Ty was pensive. I could only imagine what thoughts had to be running through his mind. Much like the bifurcated feelings I had leaving home for college, I am certain that my son is similarly conflicted. No doubt he is ecstatic to be leaving, pleased with finally being able to go home. At the same time, I am certain he is having trepidations about the trip, wondering what he would find once we made it back to Ohio.

At last, we were ready to depart. I noticed that the staff had sort of backed away from us during this final flurry. Quick farewells were shared as we settled into the van that would take us to the airport. As the latch on the hospital's closing door engaged, for us, the last time, I didn't look back. Suddenly, I realized that I was no longer lamenting what was being left behind. The door had closed. Yes, we were on our own . . . and from somewhere deep inside, I knew we'd be okay.

We were going home. Today, the first day of the rest of our lives, was unfolding in perfect fashion—just as the Universe had destined it to be.

Farewell, Craig Hospital.

A TIME FOR EVERYTHING

(October 29th)

It has been six days since our return home. The minutes of this past week have ticked away incessantly as we settle into our new lives. Adjustments are being made almost every moment as we fine-tune things to create an atmosphere conducive to Tyler's healing. This, I suspect, will be an ongoing process until at some point in time we get it right.

Charles Caleb Colton wrote: "Time is the most indefinable yet paradoxical of things; the past is gone, the future is not come, and the present becomes the past, even while we attempt to define it, and, like the flash of the lightning, at once exists and expires."

Yesterday, as I walked down our driveway toward the mailbox, I noticed what looked like a dead snake on the pavement. Upon closer scrutiny, I realized it was the remnant of a snake's skin that had been shed at an earlier time. The snake had molted its outer layer in preparation for the upcoming season.

The Gordons have molted, too. The skin we used to wear, that comfortable protective covering, has now fallen away, exposing a new layer. A tincture of time has already begun the slow process of allowing us to get acquainted with our new virgin skin.

As time has allowed this week, I've attempted to straighten up the disorder left behind months ago by our abrupt departure. There are piles of papers and stacks of clothes. Rooms are in disarray, and furniture has been displaced to accommodate Ty's new room.

Some semblance of organization has begun to slowly replace the chaos. The past four mornings, I have attempted to restart an antique windup wall clock hanging in the library. The hands remain fixed where they were when the pendulum stopped swinging almost four months ago.

Back home now, it feels as if time has stood as still as the pendulum of this old clock. Many things in the house have remained in the same position as the day of Ty's injury. Restarting the wall clock, much like the rebooting of our lives, has not been as easy as I thought. Each time I wind it up, the pendulum sleepily swings back and forth, gradually slowing until it ultimately comes to a halt. The clock seems to be saying, "No, I'm not ready to start up again. Give me just a little more time."

I don't want to delay any further, allowing more valuable time to pass. Horace Mann once wrote: "Lost, yesterday, somewhere between sunrise and sunset, two golden hours, each set with sixty diamond minutes. No reward is offered, for they are gone forever."

Watching the pendulum as it attempts to sustain its own momentum, swinging back and forth, back and forth, I envisioned a farmer of days gone by sweeping a scythe across tall grass. For years and years, he swung it at the same pace and with the same force. Then he injured his shoulder, and as hard as he tried, he could not regain his previous rhythm. He became less effective and weaker the more he persevered.

It was only when he backed off, allowing the healing process to occur, that the passage of time fostered the return of strength to the old farmer. Patience and fortitude allowed him to resume his work with an even more fluid stroke than before.

Perhaps that is the lesson for me today: there is a time for everything. I am reminded of Ecclesiastes 3:1, which I have taken the liberty of paraphrasing:

To everything, there is a season,
And a time for every purpose under heaven.
A time to be born, and a time to die;
A time to get, and a time to lose;
A time to plant, and a time to reap;
A time to weep, and a time to laugh;
A time to mourn, and a time to dance;
A time to break down, and a time to build up.

And, from the Talmud:

"He who forces time is pushed back by time; but he who
yields to time will find it to be on his side."

DON'T IT MAKE MY BROWN EYES BLUE?

(November 5th)

This morning I awoke with a suffocating darkness enveloping me. It was as if I were boxed in a tomb from which there was no escape. As I slowly forced myself to get out of bed, I realized that anger and bitterness, deep-seated emotions I had been successfully fighting off up until now, were percolating to the surface, coming to a boil. Why had God dropped me off at this place and abandoned me here? *Why have You forsaken me?* I screamed out in my mind.

As the day progressed, things only worsened, my despair deepened. I felt myself becoming more and more isolated and empty. Even though I was moving around, I felt lifeless as an overwhelming sense of help-lessness and hopelessness clutched me in its grasp. I couldn't fathom a way out of this mess.

I went through the motions of getting through the day, busying myself with various chores. I let the dog out, fed the birds, vacuumed the carpet, and mopped the kitchen floor. It wasn't until later in the day that I looked at Kavenna. He is a Burmese mountain dog and German shepherd mix. Weighing over 100 pounds, he has a gentle spirit about him. I was aware that he had been following me around all day, but I hadn't paid him much attention. It was only when I paused long enough to really look him in the eyes that I noticed the saddest look on his face.

I was perplexed. What possible reason did Kavenna have to be so sad? His life as a dog provides him with all the nourishment he needs, a comfortable place to sleep, and all the amenities of a privileged existence. Yesterday everything seemed to be okay with him. *So why the sad eyes today?* I thought. *What's wrong with you, Kavenna?*

He looked at me as if to say, "Don't you know?"

Sitting down beside him, I did something I hadn't done in the longest time. I gently began stroking his back and massaging his paws. He melted on the floor. *Kavenna* is Hawaiian for "glow in the sky." As I looked him in the eyes, I could see that today, for some reason, his radiance had vanished.

I meditated on Kavenna, contemplating what he had been through these past months. Similar to our lives, his whole world had been instantly disrupted when Angela and I departed for Denver to be with Ty. I hadn't considered the impact of such an abrupt departure on our furriest family member. I'm sure he was confused and felt abandoned, just what I was feeling now. He had no idea why we'd been gone for four months. No doubt he felt isolation as well as panic. I had ignored the fact that dogs have feelings, too.

Have you ever wondered what a dog is thinking as you bark out orders to him? When you tell him to fetch, and he looks you in the eyes while cocking his head, does your dog understand the word *fetch,* or does he sense what you're trying to communicate in another way?

These animals know when we're trying to communicate with them. Are we as receptive? At a very early age, children begin to rely on interpreting gestures from adults. Perhaps our pets do the same. Is it the sound of our voice or its inflection that imprints the commands on their minds? It may well be our body language or the energy we project, and *not* the spoken word, that results in a dog's response.

A dog is man's best friend. I think the opposite is true as well: man is a dog's best friend. After all, we have a long history with our canine companions, dating back more than 15,000 years.

This ability to connect with humans is not unique to dogs alone. A number of years ago, a raccoon behaving very strangely appeared on our property. He would come out in the daylight, atypical for creatures that tend to do their scavenging at night. One afternoon, Angela came running in from the garden yelling for me. As I ran down the stairs, she told me the raccoon, which was likely rabid, was in the garden and had staggered toward her kind of sideways, bumping into her leg.

Impulsively, I ran upstairs, unlocked my gun safe, and pulled out a shotgun, which I hadn't fired in years. As I bolted outside, the raccoon was heading away from our house, running sideways up a small hill. I aimed and prepared to shoot him. At the precise moment that my finger tensed, applying pressure on the trigger, the raccoon stopped, turned around, and looked at me. Our eyes met. In an instant, our spirits connected. His eyes conveyed to me that this was not a good day for him to die.

Slowly, I lowered the barrel as he looked at me for a moment longer. He then turned and scampered away, never to be seen again. Now, there are some who would say, "Ah, ya should've blasted the critter. He was just a sick animal with rabies." But I have come to know that every living thing is imbued with the same life force that flows through me. Just as I share my energy with everything in the Universe, everything reciprocates by sharing with me. Our hearts beat, and our energy flows collectively in harmony.

So, why the sad eyes, Kavenna? The answer was simple. He was as much a mirror to me as I was to him. On this day, he had taken on as his own the reflection of my sadness. I had unknowingly and unfairly transferred to him the negative emotions I was feeling. My companion now shared in my grief. It hung on the two of us like a rain-soaked wool blanket. That negativity would linger with us until together we'd choose to shake it off.

I made Kavenna a promise: I would try harder.

I then silently apologized that I had made his brown eyes blue.

A WALK IN THE PARK

(November 14th)

It has been more than three weeks since our return home. The dust has finally begun to settle, literally. Davo is still working diligently on the renovation, his work pace slowed by daily, earnest conversations with Ty. I assume that he's off the clock during that time . . . or maybe he should charge double!

The challenges facing us have been great, certainly no walk in the park. Thus far, the family has pulled together, overcoming every obstacle. Mattie-Rose and Laila have been godsends. Their assistance has helped us adjust to our new life. When Britt moves back home from Durango next week with Diesel, Ty's rottweiler, our family will be whole once again.

Reflecting back on the past four and a half months, I wonder how we arrived at this place in time and why each of us chose to be here. What are we to learn from the experience? Each of us will glean a different lesson that hopefully allows us to gain us a more complete understanding about ourselves and about life. How tragic it would be to endure adversity such as this without coming out of it better for having had the experience.

I have come to appreciate that the greater one's dharma—the more profound the purpose of one's life—the greater the obstacles that will be encountered along the way. To overcome these challenges, the key is how you perceive what confronts you. Everything in life is a thought. What you think of your loved ones, what you think of your job, what you think of the words in this book, what you think about a life-changing experience is simply that: your thought of that experience. And you can change the thought or the perception of something in an instant.

In my work as a cardiologist, I learned that valuable lesson many years ago. I dreaded being on call for the weekends. It was a royal pain in the arse. I'd work Monday through Friday, and then I'd be the only doctor on call for our cardiology group from Friday night through Monday morning. I would field all the calls, see all the hospitalized patients for ten cardiologists, and perform any necessary emergent heart procedures. Come Monday morning, the new week would start and I'd work again until Friday night—12 straight days!

As my weekend of on-call duty would approach, I'd become more and more depressed, a feeling that would begin to crescendo a week and a half *before* these weekends.

Realizing the futility of that mind-set, I made a conscious decision to simply change the thought. I played a game with myself. Instead of dreading the sleepless nights, instead of being upset every time my beeper went off, I convinced myself to actually look forward to the experience. I began anticipating the weekend on call as an opportunity to serve others. Every time my beeper would activate, it would signal another way for me to help someone.

And you know what happened? I had the best weekend on call in my life, all because I changed the thought. The phenomenal aspect of this was that making this shift took only a second . . . which brings me back to how I started this entry. Tyler's ordeal has certainly been anything but a walk in the park. There have been many days when I've allowed negative thoughts to percolate through my mind, dragging me down. I fight them off as best I can, not always successfully.

The other day I was on the phone with Nanny, Angela's mother. I asked her how she was doing. Her response was, "Terrible." Immediately, I was sorry I placed the call and even sorrier that I had asked her how she was doing. At that time, I was not in a very good place myself. My initial thought (thankfully not spoken) was: *Terrible? You want to see terrible? Why don't you come up and spend a day with us!*

It was then that Nanny shared with me that her only great-granddaughter, four-year-old Candace, had been hospitalized the day before with a horrible head-ache. By the next morning, she couldn't walk without staggering. The doctors at Kosair Children's Hospital discovered an inoperable brain tumor. Her long-term prognosis is not good. She will be entering a clinical trial and receiving chemo and radiation therapy.

I was stunned. I was ashamed of my judgments directed at Nanny. In an instant, every one of those negative thoughts about *our* terrible circumstance van-ished. In a split second, the thought changed. What had seemed so overwhelmingly terrible to me had be-come *a walk in the park* when compared to what baby Candace and her family are now facing.

As I petitioned the Universe on her behalf, I con-templated dharma and purpose. There is so much for us to learn on our unique spiritual journey. May God illuminate our path.

GRATITUDE

(November 26th)

Today is the 388th celebration of Thanksgiving. After landing at Plymouth Rock, the Pilgrims' first winter was a devastating one. By the beginning of the following fall, 46 of the original 102 who sailed to this continent on the Mayflower had died. The harvest of 1621 was an exceptionally bountiful one, and despite the loss of so many, the remaining colonists decided to express their gratitude by celebrating with a feast.

They knew what Melody Beattie so beautifully describes: "Gratitude unlocks the fullness of life. It turns what we have into enough, and more. It turns denial into acceptance, chaos to order, confusion to clarity. . . . Gratitude makes sense of our past, brings peace for today, and creates a vision for tomorrow."

This first Thanksgiving was not a holiday; it was simply a gathering of people who were profoundly grateful to be alive. They thanked the Almighty for the sustenance they were provided with. They appreciated their Native American brothers and sisters, who supported them during their challenging times. In fact, it wasn't until 1863 that Abraham Lincoln proclaimed Thanksgiving a national holiday to be celebrated every fourth Thursday in November.

At least once a year, Thanksgiving offers us an opportunity to pause and reflect on our many blessings. Most of us don't do this often enough. When life is cushy, we tend to settle into a comfort zone, allowing ourselves to become complacent. We forget to be thankful for all that we have, both the good fortune and what we perceive as *mis*fortune.

As Allan Knight Chalmers once said, "Crises refine life; in them you discover what you are and what you ought to do." Our family has experienced many challenges these past months, first with Ty and now with Candace. The question remains: Have they been terrible chapters in our lives, or marvelous opportunities? We could certainly choose to take the woe-is-me attitude, wallowing in our perceived suffering. Or we could use these *blessings* to achieve a more complete appreciation of life. We should be equally grateful for both the highest of peaks and the lowest of valleys; it is from them that we develop the necessary tools to help us along this journey of discovery.

It has become the Gordon Thanksgiving Day tradition that I, as the *alter cocker* (Yiddish for the oldest fart in the family), get to impart my fatherly wisdom to a captive audience at the dinner table. To the chagrin of our kids, this year will be no different.

I anticipate that any message I have to convey will be a much harder sell this year. I am certain that Ty will find it most difficult to be thankful for anything. I can only pray that he will soon come to appreciate that God spared his life for a reason, and that life is indeed very precious. I also pray that he will come to discover his dharma and then focus his entire energetic intention on that purpose.

On this Thanksgiving, I will share with my family how I'm filled with gratitude. I'm thankful that I've had five months of daily interaction with my son. I've spent quality time with him that I would not have otherwise. I give thanks daily that his life was spared. I thank God for Tyler's brilliant mind, which remains intact. I am grateful for his vital spirit, which I sense is beginning to emerge from the cocoon of darkness where it has dwelled for these past five months.

Tyler may not be feeling much gratitude on this Thanksgiving Day. He may not yet be able to walk to the dining-room table where we as a family will partake in this feast of gratitude for our many bountiful blessings. My prayer for him is that he gets to the place where he is thankful for what he has, not saddened by what he does not. I pray he will embrace that one doesn't need the disguise of legs to walk tall.

There are no accidents in the Universe . . . just the unfolding of circumstances as they are destined to be. As Leo Buscaglia so eloquently said, "Your talent is God's gift to you. What you do with it is your gift back to God."

We should be grateful every day for our many blessings. How we use them will be the noblest gauge of our thanksgiving.

K-I-S-S

(December 14th)

This morning I witnessed what appeared to be a miracle. At first light, I looked out at the lake and saw our swans walking on water! I thought to myself, *Wow! They must have experienced some sort of epiphany during the night, as just yesterday they were paddling around the lake like normal birds.*

When the gray skies brightened a bit, I realized the optical illusion of the miracle. Through the frigid night, nature had deposited a thin layer of ice on part of the surface of our lake, a layer so smooth that it appeared to be fluid. The swans were actually walking on thin ice. How natural they looked as they waddled across the silvery surface. As I pondered their feat, I acknowledged that I too have been walking on thin ice these past several months—although I don't believe that I've pulled off the act as well as the swans appeared to be on this crisp autumn morning.

As more daylight appeared, I could distinguish the lines of separation between ice and water. In fact, there were six *S*-shaped lines, to be exact. Some were large, others smaller. I meditated on the *S*'s. What was the lesson this consonant was trying to teach me?

It then occurred to me that the reason there were six was obvious: one for each member of our immediate family. As I made the *S* sound over and over again, the meaning slowly came to me.

The accumulating weight of responsibilities in life, whether related to work, finances, or relationships can be formidable—and at times overwhelming. In attempting to manage, many individuals may feel like they're walking on thin ice. If the burden becomes too heavy, the fragile surface fractures and they lose their footing. For some, the burden falls from their backs, allowing themselves to be rescued from the frigid waters. For others, bound tightly to their baggage, the weight drags them under as they sink deeper into the cold darkness below the surface.

Meditating on the *S*'s, what came to mind was *K-I-S-S*. It was not the band or the touching of lips. It was just those four letters.

Then it hit me. Years ago my good friend Don Karas, a colleague at The Heart Group, made an insightful observation. Every year he, Tyler, and I would put together a band for Docs Who Rock, a United Way fund-raiser. Each year, the presentation became more grandiose and extravagant—we sure performed some crazy antics! When things got too wild, Don would always implore me to "K-I-S-S." No, he wasn't putting the moves on me; he was merely suggesting for me to **K**eep **I**t **S**imple, **S**tupid. And he was right. The more complicated our presentation, the less successful it became.

Hence, the lesson of the *S*'s etched in the thin ice this morning: keep life simple. As Sir Winston Churchill explained, "Out of intense complexities intense simplicities emerge."

Despite the fact that challenges may appear to be very complicated, in truth they are not. By keeping it simple, living one day at a time, tackling one problem at a time, and distilling things down to the basics, we can meet those seemingly overwhelming obstacles with greater success.

I'LL BE HOME FOR CHRISTMAS

(December 25th)

Christmas has always held a special place in my heart, which I know may sound strange coming from someone raised in the Jewish faith. Yes, Hanukah always occurred around the same time, but it was Christmas that made the season special for me. For many of my friends and acquaintances, Jesus's birthday was a holy one. It represented a time when almost everyone forgot his or her differences, if only for one day. I remember reading that even during World War II the German and Allied forces stopped fighting on Christmas Day. Strange how enemies who worship the same God can put aside differences just to celebrate a birthday!

I recall the serenity of one especially blissful, wintry Christmas Eve. I had gone out for a long walk by myself.

The snow's fluffy blanket, already five inches deep, continued to grow as snowflakes gently descended upon the quiet landscape. I do not recall ever experiencing a purer peace than on that solitary late-evening walk years ago. The entire world was nestled quietly in a tranquil cocoon of white cashmere. It was one of those "Kodak moments" in life. I occasionally find myself reaching back to that place of serenity, to a time when life seemed easier.

CHRISTMAS IS THE CELEBRATION OF THE BIRTH OF BABY JESUS, physically born into the material plane. In the Christian faith, to be born again refers to a spiritual rebirth, a re-dedication to a new path leading toward salvation. From Ezekiel 36:26: "And I will give you a new heart, and a new spirit I will put within you." In essence, rebirth offers a radical change of heart and direction.

It has been 179 days since Ty was born again. I describe his rebirth not in the sense of becoming a part of the Christian faith; rather, in finding oneself on a new and quite different path—one that will, in similar fashion, require a dramatic change of heart.

Perhaps these two descriptions of being born again are one and the same. "Seeing the light" has been variably described by many of the world's religions as first recognizing and then achieving what is referred to as God-consciousness, Buddha-consciousness, or Christ-consciousness. Those states involve a change of thought, a rebirth into a new paradigm on the enlightened nature of growth. It is a universal goal.

For 30 years, the Gordons have made the annual trek home to "Tucky" for the holidays. For months we would anticipate the reunion of souls with our family. When we crossed the Kentucky state line, we'd cheer as I'd honk the car horn announcing our arrival back in the Bluegrass state. While all four of our children were born north of the Mason-Dixon Line in Ohio, they have always referred to "Tucky" as going home.

And so, why should this year be any different? Why shouldn't we go home? I questioned whether to continue the tradition of our annual trip. Ty's special needs posed daunting logistical challenges. I vacillated up until the moment of our departure from Richfield, but depart we did.

The six of us made it to Kentucky without so much as a hiccup. We arrived safely in Georgetown, settled in to a new environment, and created a comfort zone we all could enjoy.

The reconnection with family has been a beautiful experience.

As usual, everyone but me stays up until the wee hours of the night. During this time of year, I would guess it is in anticipation of catching a glimpse of Old Saint Nick. On Christmas morning, with everyone still snuggled into bed at 5:30, I had the chance to sit by myself on the couch in Nanny's living room and take in the beauty of her glorious white Christmas tree. The limbs were gilded with fluffy snow and adorned with angels—all of them smiling down on me from their perches.

Often, memories are evoked by a certain fragrance, a sound, or even a thought. This morning, I revisited that special Christmas Eve of many years ago, the silent night I enjoyed walking alone in the deep snow. For a moment, I was back in that place and time of absolute serenity, reveling in the beauty of nature, embracing what Source provides to us all if we open our souls to it. It is, after all, what we all strive for . . . peace, shalom, salaam.

Yes, the Gordons made it home for Christmas. I pray that each of you can do the same—if not in the physical sense, in the spiritual one. May God bless us, everyone!

DOES ANYBODY REALLY KNOW WHAT TIME IT IS?

(January 1st, 2010)

Yesterday, we safely made the trip back up to Ohio. As we pulled into our driveway, it began to snow, continuing through the night.

When I arose this morning, everyone else was still awake. They are now nestled in various cozy spots around the house. Ty is in his room, Laila and Britt in another bedroom. Mattie-Rose and Angela have crashed on the sofa. I pray each of their slumbers will be peaceful and rejuvenating.

It is the dawn of a new day, a new year, a new decade. I must admit that the day started for me tumultuously, which was my own fault of course. To calm down, I joined nature's blanket of snow for a walk in the woods, embracing the silence. In a leafless tree near our home, I noticed an abandoned bird's nest. It was filled to the brim with freshly fallen snow and capped at an off angle that was created by the wind blowing past the remnants of what in a different season had been home to a family of birds.

I contemplated that empty nest. Last year at this time, Angela and I were empty nesters. I remember last year thinking about *our* little birdies—Mattie-Rose, Laila, Britt, and Tyler—flapping their maturing wings. I wondered where their travels would take them. Deep down, I hoped they would find their way back home to our nest. I knew, of course, that most little birdies do not return home; they make their own nests and hatch their own little birdies that then also fly away. Such is the way of life.

As I continued my communion with nature, a flock of blackbirds flew toward me, one bird leading the way. The direction of flight taken by the flock changed from moment to moment, circuitously swerving one way then, in an instant, changing course at the whim of the leader. I wondered if the lead bird really knew where it was going. It's an enormous responsibility to lead a flock. I know. You see, I *am* that bird, and the flock is my family.

Do I know exactly where I am leading them? The answer to that question is an unequivocal no. Although I have an idea of where we should go, getting there remains a serious challenge.

The flock of blackbirds landed on the branches of a nearby tree. I noticed one of them in particular. It was perched on one of the lower branches and had a damaged claw. It was disfigured, gnarled, and contracted due to an injury or frostbite. But there it was, balancing on its good leg. Although this bird wasn't in the best of shape, it obviously remained an active participant of this family, joining the flock as best it could as they continued on their journey. I was reminded of this quote by Henry Van Dyke: "[T]he woods would be very silent if no birds sang there except those that sang best."

As if on cue from the leader, the flock took flight. The bird with the damaged claw took off, albeit not as gracefully as the rest. Away they went, becoming a twisting and careening mass of black flying farther and farther from me until they were out of sight.

Watching their departure, it occurred to me that birds don't celebrate New Year's Day. I'm certain they don't waste their energy making resolutions they cannot or will not keep. They likely have no conception of a minute, an hour, or a day. After all, time is our own concoction. Whether it's the ticking of a clock, witnessing daylight transition to nightfall, watching as winter becomes spring, or acknowledging that years meld into centuries, time is our way of cataloging experiences, placing them in neat little slots, New Year's Day being one.

Just as quickly as the flock of blackbirds departed, this past year has flown by. It came and went in the blink of an eye. During these past 12 months, lives have changed dramatically. Some birdies left their nest, while others returned home. Miracles occurred. A very large "bird," US Airways flight 1549, landed safely in the Hudson River; and another "bird" recently remained in flight after a failed attempt by terrorists to bring it down. Despite a mechanical malfunction, Tyler Gordon has remained in flight as well. There is much to be thankful for.

One might choose to separate one year from the next. Or, like the blackbirds, consider this transition as simply the continuation of one timeless moment into another. Instead of Happy New Year, may I wish you a Happy New Now.

MAGIC CARPET RIDE

(March 5th)

We have traveled to many destinations while on our journey. Some were near; others took us to faraway lands. Some of the places were bathed in light; others were not. Many seemed strangely familiar, some terribly foreign.

This morning, I awoke to glorious sunshine. I was out for a walk, when I noticed a hawk soaring high in the clear blue skies above me. I marveled at how it glided so effortlessly in the sky.

Have you ever wondered how a bird such as a condor manages to stay aloft all day long without so much as a flap of its wings? These magnificent, aerodynamically gifted creatures have learned the technique of taking advantage of the natural atmosphere and updrafts in order to conserve energy. Thermals, as they're called, form as the rays of sunshine stream through the cool morning air, heating the earth's surface. Pockets of hot air rise and are held in place for a while by layers of colder air from above. Catching one of these rising thermals with outstretched wings, some birds are able to glide effortlessly. The only energy that must be expended is in making minor steering adjustments.

Don't you wish you could fly? In our dreams, perhaps, we have succeeded in defying the pull of gravity, lifting off into flight. How exhilarating it would be to have the capability to just fly away, leaving behind whatever troubled you. With the flap of your wings, you could escape the realities of life. It would be even more expedient if we had at our beck and call a magic carpet that could transport us instantaneously away from our tribulations and take us to any destination we desire. Much like the legendary stories of *Arabian Nights,* our flying carpet would catch the wind lifting us up. Like the wings of the condor, it would effortlessly carry us off to peaceful places.

OUR FAMILY HAS BEEN ON ITS OWN magic-carpet ride these past eight months. Our flying carpet has carried us to faraway and foreign places we never dreamed existed. Our bird's-eye view of the terrain has blessed us with a perspective not many individuals get the opportunity to experience.

What one sees is based on perception. Even our beautiful magic carpet can be viewed from two vantage points. Looking at it from the underside, all that can be seen are the burlap strings that hold it together. The view from the top, however, shows us quite beautiful designs of intricately woven patterns. Seated on the carpet, the Gordons have appreciated its beauty, all the while learning the lessons offered by our travels.

And when our joyride comes to an end and we gently touch down at our final destination, the anticipation is that our magic-carpet ride will have fulfilled its promise, safely delivering us to the place where miracles manifest.

Lately, I've had a recurring dream. In it, there's a knock at my door. Tyler comes walking in with a definite bounce in his step. It's as if none of this has happened. He walks in with such confidence that I'm astounded. Knowing that he can walk again, the emotions I feel are indescribable.

Ah! What dreams may come when the fantasy sets you free! Imagination provides the vehicle; the magic-carpet ride takes us to the place where powerful healing can occur. Giddyup, magic carpet. Onward, upward, higher and higher . . .

LETTING GO

(April 25th)

Why is it that when it begins to rain we run for cover? This morning, the sky was dreary and dark, over-cast with gray clouds weighed down by moisture. One could feel in the air that a downpour was coming. I was sitting near a blue spruce looking out at the lake when I first felt one raindrop—and then, in an instant, thou-sands of drops came falling from the heavens.

Instinctively, I started to bolt back to the protection of our home. Yet then I felt a strong call to stay right where I was. Within this rainstorm, a truth was about to unfold for me.

I was a silent participant, a witness to nature, im-mersed in the white noise created by the rain. I flashed back to my conversation with God on the flight to Den-ver so many months ago. In the tranquility of this white noise, I once again connected to a deeper dimension of knowing, a place where truth becomes clear.

The two young swans on our lake have never witnessed the building of a nest or their parents' rituals surrounding their births. And yet, somehow, they know just what to do to perpetuate their species.

Most people envision these animals as majestic and docile, gracefully and effortlessly skimming across the top of still waters. Not during this season! When nesting season begins, the male becomes quite aggressive. He will incessantly chase interlopers from *his* territory. This morning, a pair of Canada geese had intruded into his domain. He then fluffed his feathers, making himself appear much larger. In this commanding costume, he chased the geese for well over an hour, undeterred by the downpour of rain. The more agile and adept geese were able to avoid the swan's aggressiveness by staying at least one step (or wing flap) ahead of him.

It seemed to me that the swan's time might be better spent building a nest rather than expending so much energy chasing off the geese. If he could just make room in his mind for these uninvited guests and accept their landing rights on our lake, life would be more peaceful, and likely more productive.

I was distracted from the swan dance by a rustling in a tree. A mourning dove had built a nest on one of the lower limbs. She peered down at me, wondering what the intentions were of this intruder.

A male dove landed near the nest, and I assumed he was her mate. I was expecting him to come after me, when another male nose-dived toward the first male, chasing him off. The second one was actually the mate, and he was going through the same ritual as the swan in his attempts at protecting his domain from trespassers.

A few moments later, there was a commotion in the pachysandra ground cover next to me. I could see two separate movements in the leaves; both were heading in the same direction, one right behind the other. I followed the cascade of moving leaves as the disturbance on the ground coursed to an opening from which ran two chipmunks, one chasing after the other. They, too, were engaged in the same territorial protectionism.

When I see a sequence of such seemingly unrelated events, I know that there is a deeper meaning for me to contemplate. It's usually the Divine saying, "Okay, Terry, pay attention. There is something important here for you to learn."

Territoriality came to mind. With egos blazing, these creatures expended so much of their precious energy fluffing their feathers. They were hoarding what they perceived to exclusively belong to them, as if their territory should remain theirs forever. But life is not like that. Nothing remains unchanged; everything is transient and impermanent. Each creature must learn to appreciate what it has while it lasts, but be ready to give it up when it's time. We shouldn't be sad because it's over; we should be thankful that it was there in the first place.

Human beings often go through a similar territorial dance with one another, or even within ourselves. With our egos ruffling our feathers, we grasp on to what we hope will never change, physical stuff such as our nests or our bodies. We're reluctant to accept the transitory nature of the material plane. Despite the natural aging process, an illness, or a spinal-cord injury, we want our bodies to remain unchanged. Our egos, attempting to preserve the familiar past, create an illusory facade that only promotes suffering and fosters turmoil that will linger until such time we decide to let it go. The more we hold on to this false sense of security, the less secure we become. And, like mercury, the harder we squeeze it, the greater the likelihood that it will slip right through our fingers. So it is with what we perceive as "ours." We are no different from the male swan that expended so much energy protecting his domain.

As the rainstorm gently abated, the white noise gave way to silence. As a beautiful rainbow gently arced across the sky, this lesson from Lao-tzu came to me: "When I let go of what I am, I become what I might be."

Life is like crossing a set of monkey bars. You can choose to just hang there, but in order to move forward, you'll eventually have to let go.

CELEBRATE
ME HOME

(May 4th)

Relatively calm waters have prevailed these past several months. The tumultuous roller-coaster ride had leveled off a bit . . . that is, until this morning. In an instant, *kaboom!* Pent-up anger erupted from Tyler like a volcano spewing molten rock.

Anger can be a slow suicide of the soul. Its effect is destructive, usurping vital energy from its bearer. From *A Course in Miracles:* "Those who attack do not *know* they are blessed. They attack because they believe they are *deprived.* Give therefore of *your* abundance and teach your brothers *theirs.*" And also: "Every loving thought is true. Everything else is an appeal for healing and help. . . . Can anyone be justified in responding with anger to a brother's plea for help?"

I constantly remind myself of the wise Native American who said that in order to understand where a man is coming from, you must first walk a few miles in his moccasins. Even though I live with Tyler and see what he endures daily, the truth is that I cannot fathom what he's actually going through. Although I ache when I see his spirit sink deeper into despair, it's impossible for me to don his moccasins, to view life completely from his perspective.

I must admit, at times I have allowed his brief episodes of anger to get to me. On occasion, my ego rebounds in opposition to his verbal challenges. But in this, I've gleaned invaluable insight. I've learned that I should not judge my son for misdirected anger born of his immense suffering.

His rage has taught me two important lessons: restraint and humility. I've become adept at defusing the anger and resentment he occasionally expresses. In effect, I take it from him without accepting the gift.

There's a story about a man who went to see the Buddha with the sole purpose of attempting to anger him. The man believed that not even the Buddha could possibly be at peace *all* the time. For three days, the man treated the Enlightened One rudely. He cursed at him, treated him with disrespect, and even spat on him. Despite the appalling treatment, the Buddha remained in perfect, loving peace, not responding to the man's verbal and physical attacks.

When the three days were up, the man approached, apologizing for his actions. He asked, "How is it that for three days as I treated you like the lowliest of the low, you were able to maintain your ever-peaceful presence?"

The Buddha contemplated the question, and then replied, "It is quite simple. If someone gives you a gift and you don't accept it, to whom does the gift belong?"

When Ty vents his frustration at me, I've learned to refuse the gift of anger by becoming transparent. Rather than responding or reacting to his harsh words, I simply feel them pass through me unimpeded. I don't oppose the anger or direct it back toward him. I yield to it, allowing it to flow freely through me. I neutralize the poison within his anger, bathing it in my unconditional love. I let it pass through me on its outward journey into the Universe.

To facilitate this process, I commune with nature, which is a grounding experience that offers me the serenity of solitude and provides the environment for deep introspection. I usually come back from the meditation carrying something worth remembering.

Respite this morning came with a solitary hike through the forest near our home. I have walked this comfortable path many times. During this time alone, it's just me in this piece of heaven and at one with nature. It is truly blissful.

As I walked along the worn and rutted path leading away from our lake, I could see sun-mottled woods ahead. I enjoyed the glistening sunlight as it filtered through the canopy of leaves, bathing the plush emerald foliage on the ground below. Birds were chirping, their musical vibrato bidding each other a good morning. I passed two small saplings whose close branches formed the perfect setting for a spider's web. Dew clung to the gossamer's delicate strands, and it sparkled in the early-morning sunlight like diamonds on a necklace.

Off in the distance, I heard a woodpecker searching for food, his staccato pecking reverberating throughout the woods. The relaxing sonata of nature unfolded before my senses and relieved the tension in my neck and shoulders.

Veering from the path, I heard a song beneath my feet as I trod on the trees' foliage from years gone by. The tall trees loomed above, their thick canopy now muting the sun. Suddenly, they shivered in the wind

. . . which then cascaded down toward me, covering my body in a wave of gooseflesh.

A small critter, frightened by my intrusion, scurried from the underbrush and scampered farther from the path. I picked up my pace attempting to follow. Every so often, he would stop and look back in my direction, as if beckoning, enticing me to follow him deeper into the woods.

An occasional crackling of twigs beneath my feet resounded in the silence. Soon, all I could hear was the sound of my footfalls on the thick forest floor. I looked around and suddenly realized that I didn't know where I was. Warped trees, deep underbrush, and vines entwined me in their constricting coils. Thorny brambles sliced at the skin on my arms as I began to run. Ducking and weaving past branches, I frantically tried to escape.

I ran aimlessly, disoriented. My heart was racing, my breathing intensified as adrenaline surged through my veins. Realizing the futility of this approach, I came to an exhausted halt. Spinning around 360 degrees, every direction I faced looked the same. I was lost. It was terrifying!

I stood there panting, trying to catch my breath and gather my thoughts. I listened for any cues, any hints for me to follow. I even longed for the tiny creature that had scampered across my path earlier. There was silence, deafening silence.

If only I were the Jolly Green Giant, I'd be able to tower above this strangling mass of bushes and plants. If I could climb to the treetops or just find some high ground, I could rise above and figure out how to find my way out of this tangle. Then I would be saved. . . .

I heard a rustling. I was not alone! It was a gray owl high in the branches of the tallest tree. From his perch, he could see where I needed to go. This guiding spirit arrived at just the right moment to show me the way. With a powerful and graceful motion, this creature swooped down to make sure he had my attention. I followed. He effortlessly rose from the lowest branches to the highest ones.

I followed his lead as faint rays of sun began streaming down from above, revealing themselves to me once again. Higher he flew, flapping his wings until all at once we both reached a high clearing where the canopy of trees no longer obstructed my view. The owl's watchful eye still affixed on me, he floated above, circling one last time. Seeing that I was safely on my way, he spread his dazzling wings and vanished into the horizon.

The comforting rays of the sun caressed me with their warmth. I had made it back home. As I walked up the hill toward our house, the lesson I was to learn became clear: Tyler remains entangled in his own under-brush. He cannot yet see the way out of his quagmire.

I was sent here to scout for him. When the time is right, when Tyler is ready, I will help to celebrate him home, to a place where peace abounds. Until that day, just like my guiding owl, I will soar to those rarified places in the heavens from where guidance comes, returning to circle patiently in close orbit with my son until I'm certain he reaches a place where he too can see the beauty of a new morning's horizon.

Tyler's journey is far from over. I will keep the promise made to him so many years ago as I sang him to sleep with "Cody's Song" by Kenny Loggins:

> *There's so much to learn,*
> *And when you want me*
> *Then I'll show you. . . .*
>
> *I'll be there to sing to you,*
> *I promise you*
> *I promise to*
> *Comfort you and sing to you.*
>
> *And darlin' I'll be there*
> *Anytime and anywhere,*
> *Tyler, I'll be there . . . just for you.*

I love you, son.

EPILOGUE

And so, the journey continues.

Rabbi David Horowitz once imparted this wisdom to me: "Each of us travels through life on our own unique path. Perhaps we have a particular goal or destination in mind. But what we find is that often the trip itself teaches us more than we might have ever expected. The journey becomes more important than reaching the ultimate destination."

Moses and the Israelites traveled in the desert for more than 40 years. They certainly could have found their way much sooner, but it was not destined to be. Theirs was a journey of discovery and maturation. Many lessons needed to be learned before they could enter the Promised Land. Their ordeal was more about strengthening the people than it was the settlement of the land.

Similar to the journey of the Israelites, that of the Gordons has seemed like a 40-year trek. We have learned much about each other, ourselves, and life. We have shared great sadness and experienced moments of exhilaration. Along the way, there have been times of famine where we hungered for solace and peace. On our often-desolate path, we have thirsted for knowledge. Yet we have persevered. We have endured. And as a result, we have grown and matured. We are better for having had the experience.

The falls of our life have indeed given us the energy to propel ourselves to a place of much higher consciousness. God has never once left our side. I am certain His Divine presence will remain with us as we continue along our way through yet unchartered terrain. What lies ahead, only our Guide knows. It is certain we'll encounter more thunderclouds. But these too shall pass, for in God's creative wisdom . . . *no storm lasts forever.*

Namaste.

ABOUT THE AUTHOR

Dr Terry A. Gordon graduated from Emory University with a degree in psychology. Having completed his medical-school training at the Kansas City College of Osteopathic Medicine, a rotating internship at Doctors Hospital, and internal-medicine training at Akron General Medical Center, he then completed his invasive-cardiology fellowship at the Cleveland Clinic. He is board certified in both internal medicine and cardiovascular diseases.

One of his missions in life is saving the lives of our most precious resource, our children. When Terry was president of the Summit County, Ohio, American Heart Association, he led a campaign to place automated external defibrillators (AEDs) in every junior high and high school following the tragic death of Josh Miller, a 15-year-old football player at Barberton High School. For Terry's efforts, the American Heart Association named him the National Physician of the Year in 2002.

He is currently spearheading a national campaign: the goal is to place one defibrillator in every single school in America. The bill is called the Josh Miller HEARTS Act.

Now retired from the practice of cardiology, Terry's purpose in life is to continue serving by giving himself away every day. He does so by sharing with others his insight to what we all desire: peace, shalom and salaam.

www.drterrygordon.com

We hope you enjoyed this Hay House book. If you'd
like to receive our online catalog featuring additional
information on Hay House books and products, or if you'd
like to find out more about the Hay Foundation, please contact:

Hay House UK, Ltd., 292B Kensal Rd., London W10 5BE
Phone: 0-20-8962-1230 • Fax: 0-20-8962-1239
www.hayhouse.co.uk • **www.hayfoundation.org**

Published and distributed in the United States by: Hay House, Inc.,
P.O. Box 5100, Carlsbad, CA 92018-5100 • Phone: (1) 760 431-
7695 or (1) 800 654-5126 • Fax: (1) 760 431-6948 or
(1) 800 650-5115 • www.hayhouse.com®

Published and distributed in Australia by: Hay House Australia Pty.
Ltd., 18/36 Ralph St., Alexandria NSW 2015 • *Phone:*
612-9669-4299 • *Fax:* 612-9669-4144 • www.hayhouse.com.au

Published and distributed in the Republic of South Africa by:
Hay House SA (Pty), Ltd., P.O. Box 990, Witkoppen 2068
Phone/Fax: 27-11-467-8904 • www.hayhouse.co.za

Published in India by: Hay House Publishers India, Muskaan
Complex, Plot No. 3, B-2, Vasant Kunj, New Delhi 110 070 • *Phone:*
91-11-4176-1620 • *Fax:* 91-11-4176-1630 • www.hayhouse.co.in

Distributed in Canada by: Raincoast, 9050 Shaughnessy St.,
Vancouver, B.C. V6P 6E5 • *Phone:* (604) 323-7100
Fax: (604) 323-2600 • www.raincoast.com

Take Your Soul on a Vacation

Visit **www.HealYourLife.com**® to regroup, recharge,
and reconnect with your own magnificence. Featuring blogs,
mind-body-spirit news, and life-changing wisdom
from Louise Hay and friends.

Visit **www.HealYourLife.com** today!

NOTES

NOTES

NOTES

NOTES